SocietyNow

SocietyNow: short, informed books, explaining why our world is the way it is, now.

The *SocietyNow* series provides readers with a definitive snapshot of the events, phenomena and issues that are defining our twenty-first century world. Written by leading experts in their fields, and publishing as each subject is being contemplated across the globe, titles in the series offer a thoughtful, concise and rapid response to the major political and economic events and social and cultural trends of our time.

SocietyNow makes the best of academic expertise accessible to a wider audience, to help readers untangle the complexities of each topic and make sense of our world the way it is, now.

The Trump Phenomenon: How the Politics of Populism Won in 2016
Peter Kivisto

Becoming Digital: Towards a Post-Internet Society
Vincent Mosco

Understanding Brexit: Why Britain Voted to Leave the European Union
Graham Taylor

Selfies: Why We Love (and Hate) Them
Katrin Tiidenberg

Internet Celebrity: Understanding Fame Online
Crystal Abidin

Corbynism: A Critical Approach
Matt Bolton and Frederick Harry Pitts

KARDASHIAN KULTURE

How Celebrities Changed Life in the 21st Century

BY

ELLIS CASHMORE

United Kingdom – North America – Japan
India – Malaysia – China

Emerald Publishing Limited
Howard House, Wagon Lane, Bingley BD16 1WA, UK

First edition 2019

Reprints and permissions service
Contact: permissions@emeraldinsight.com

British Library Cataloguing in Publication Data
A catalogue record for this book is available from the British
Library

ISBN: 978-1-78743-707-4 (Print)
ISBN: 978-1-78743-706-7 (Online)
ISBN: 978-1-78743-964-1 (Epub)

ISOQAR certified
Management System,
awarded to Emerald
for adherence to
Environmental
standard
ISO 14001:2004.

Certificate Number 1985
ISO 14001

INVESTOR IN PEOPLE

CONTENTS

ACKNOWLEDGEMENTS

My work with Jamie Cleland and Kevin Dixon, in *Screen Society*, along with my solo books *Elizabeth Taylor: A Private Life for Public Consumption*, and *Making Sense of Sports*, have informed several passages of this book.

CHAPTER 1

MIRACULOUS ENGAGEMENT

You probably haven't heard of Dorje Mingma. He was a Nepalese Sherpa assisting a Swiss expedition to climb Mount Everest. On October 31, 1952, he was killed by falling ice and buried in the windless basin known as the Valley of Silence. Dorje Mingma was the last mountaineer to die trying to climb Everest, before the alp was finally conquered in the following year by Edmund Hillary and Tenzing Norgay, whose names are much more familiar.

Anna Nicole Smith died in 2007. The comparison may be tenuous, but the last person to fail and perish before an acclaimed triumph is usually forgotten. Smith was a *Playboy* centerfold, a model for Guess Jeans, occasional actor, diet products' endorser and sometime reality show star who was nearly-but-not-quite famous for being famous.

Born Vickie Lynn Hogan in Mexia, Texas in 1967, she married at 17 and had a son. Her idol was Marilyn Monroe. Working as a pole dancer at Gigi's, a strip club in Houston, in 1991, she caught the eye of a customer, who, according to *Forbes* (March 4, 2013), offered her $4,000 a month for 'consulting.' He was J. Howard Marshall II, a recently widowed oil billionaire. In 1994, the uncommon couple married; he was

89 and Smith was 26. Within 14 months, Marshall was dead, leaving behind an estate valued at $1.6 billion.

Smith made no secret of her desire to be at the center of public scrutiny. Once asked if the generous media coverage she received after her relationship with Marshall became known bothered her, she laughed: 'Oh, no, I like it ... I love the paparazzi. They take pictures and I just smile away. I've always liked attention.'

This probably gave away her game: she practically invited the media into her life, rarely missing the chance to turn a photo opportunity into a fiasco; she'd guzzle champagne from the bottle, flash her ample breasts and behave amorously with both women and men. Her exhibitionism knew no bounds. And the plot in which she featured made onlookers indignant or sympathetic, but probably not much in-between; she was what we often call a divisive figure − someone who causes disagreement between people. Of course, this made her a great narrative: blonde, white-trash gold-digger, who parties like an airstrike, splattering anyone in range, drops lucky and marries one of the richest men in America months before he croaks.

Even better, in 2002, the E! network capitalized on what was then the embryonic new TV genre, the reality show, by launching *The Anna Nicole Show*. This chronicled the minutiae of her everyday life, like visiting the dentist and feeding her dog, Sugar Pie, Prozac. The series ended in 2004. Smith also featured in advertisements for TrimSpa, a diet supplement. In 2006, she gave birth to a daughter and, in a dreadful twist of fate, Smith's son from her first marriage died while visiting her and the new baby in the Bahamas. Cause of death: lethal interaction of methadone and antidepressants.

A long-running legal case seesawed until 2006 when the US Supreme Court ruled in a way that appeared to open the way for Smith to receive over $450 million from her ex-husband's estate, though she died on February 8, 2007, from an accidental overdose, without seeing a penny. In June the same year, Paris Hilton started her prison sentence. Everyone, it seemed, was talking about her. She was Hillary to Smith's Mingma; everybody knows the former, but not many remember the latter, who came close, but failed.

Smith was ahead of her time – not by much, but enough to prevent her capitalizing on the new fascination for celebrities. She embodied all the basic or intrinsic qualities of the new type of celebrity. But in the mid-1990s, there were no reality TV shows (at least not by that name), nor the promotional apparatus to handle putatively talentless personalities and no public with sufficient curiosity to become ensorcelled by someone who appeared to be just a Marilyn manqué. Then, a butterfly flapped its wings and set in motion a connecting sequence of events that delivered seismic activity.

When in 2003 Barbra Streisand learned that an aerial photograph of her California beach house was among 12,000 pictures uploaded to the internet as part of a collection, she did what any self-respecting Academy Award-winning artist, with ecstatically reviewed Broadway and West End shows, more number one albums than any other woman and over 50 million records sold, would do: she sued. After all, she was *la prima diva*: temperamental perhaps, and rumored to be difficult to please. Streisand is said to have demanded that all hotel staff at the MGM Grand in Las Vegas enter and leave her room backwards and not make eye contact (even Queen Elizabeth permits gawping). Watching her 1991 film *Prince of Tides* on TV, Streisand considered the commercials too loud, so she hotlined NBC television to tell them to turn it down, allegedly.

So, when the California Coastal Records Project, which maintains an online photographic archive of almost the entire California coastline, reproduced images that included shots of her Malibu mansion, Streisand objected the action violated her privacy. The problem was that Streisand's legal move was generously publicized and her attempt to suppress the pictures paradoxically encouraged a half-million people to rush to their computers to look at her home online. It was an explosive backfire and a case that introduced a new phrase into our lexicon: the Streisand Effect, when an attempt to prevent something actually causes it to happen, like the butterfly that stops fluttering to try to prevent an earthquake.

There was another less well-known but more apocalyptic meaning secreted in the Streisand affair: it blew apart the concept of privacy. If someone as illustrious, and revered as Streisand, with money, influence and status couldn't get her own way, who could? Two years before, she might have prevailed. But by 2003, the net was undergoing a kind of democratization. The piece of technology known as Web 2.0 was changing the internet from a source of information into a fully interactive platform. Users were able to communicate with each other and create text, images or videos – what we later called memes – which they could then share with others. The newly social nature of the internet effectively meant it became lawless. If the pictures of Streisand's home were online, there was nothing she could do in practical terms to stop people looking at them. Audiences had control. Initially, this disturbed, later provoked and still later challenged, not just A-listers like Streisand but anyone who sought fame. Actually, it changed all of us.

There's an invisible filament joining this event to Kim Kardashian. People idolize her almost as much as she seems to idolize herself, but without quite knowing why (well, maybe she knows something we don't). She's uncoupled greatness from achievement in the sense that she is acknowledged as one of the best known and distinct women in the world; she has a certain eminence and creates an aura with her presence, yet boasts few tangible achievements beyond her own gravitational sphere. She appears and sells stuff, but not much else. Not even film turkeys, flopped records or remaindered books (her sole contribution to literature, a 2015 book called *Selfish*, sold decently). Then there is the feeling of intimacy with others who are, at once, proximate and remote. Other celebrities of the twenty-first century had created bonds of digital familiarity but none had exploited the possibilities offered by the post-Web 2.0 interactivity more fully than Kardashian and her family. When audiences were drawn to the twitter feeds of Rihanna, Lady Gaga and Britney Spears in the 2000s, Kim Kardashian was learning from Paris Hilton, observing how her mentor was able to keep pace with entertainers who had what could be described as traditional talents.

Kim and her family were sovereign and unrivaled for their craft and ingenuity. If they'd surfaced in, say, the 1990s, it's possible to imagine they would have been greeted with shrieks of derision and dismissed as unwholesomely talentless, self-adoring exhibitionists. Correction: they probably wouldn't be greeted with anything at all; more likely, the whole family would be totally ignored while audiences trained their attentions on the likes of Madonna and Michael Jackson, artists who somehow managed to provoke and disturb audiences and produce entertainment of the first magnitude.

Later, Kim Kardashian produced entertainment; in fact, she fascinated people, though exactly how and why was not abundantly clear. But in 2007, the year when *Keeping Up With the Kardashians* started on TV, something comparable to 9/11 was happening to culture. I don't wish to overstate unpleasant similarities; the date of the attack on New York's World Trade Center in 2001 is a singular event and among its manifold consequences was a pervasive awareness that the most deadly weapon was also the most basic – life itself. Suicide attacks characterized an era in which conventional wisdom on just about everything was exchanged for an admission that we knew little.

We know little about what we've decided to call celebrity culture. People still scratch their heads and wonder about Kim Kardashian; she gives her best performances by doing almost nothing. And we act as if we're mesmerized by her and her relatives. As the post-9/11 mood reminded us we knew little, the epoch ushered in by the Kardashians prompts us to wonder whether we even know the right questions to ask, never mind the answers. 'Why is she famous?' has an obvious answer: no woman in history has ever been afforded such lavish media coverage. Maybe Diana, Princess of Wales. But we'll save that argument. For now, Kim Kardashian is never out of the media. And we continue to scratch our heads. This is a woman from a family we know about basically from watching them sitting on sofas, eating salads and taking pictures of themselves.

Celebrity culture, as we know it in this century, may be momentary. Our fascination with renown may not last much longer. But there are no signs that it's fading; quite the reverse – new areas of society are being affected. Politics, religion, the arts and public health have all been substantially changed by our unprecedented obsession with the famous. In fact, it's impossible to discern one aspect of culture today that hasn't been affected. We've changed.

Kim Kardashian and her relatives aren't wholly responsible for this, of course. Nor is anyone or anything in particular. Celebrity culture might seem as if it's the result of some playful gods attempting a mischievous experiment. Like the celestial beings in the heavens as visualized in the 1936 Lothar Mendes film of the HG Wells story from 1898, *The Man Who Could Work Miracles*. 'Can't you leave these nasty little creatures alone?' one deity asks another who is looking down on Earth contemplating and granting humans extraordinary powers. 'Their lives are so short, their efforts so feeble ... I'm going to give them all power.'

'What will happen if these silly greedy human scabs who only breed and scramble spread out among our stars?' asks his divine colleague, who persuades him to limit his gift to a few mortals. He eventually sees sense: 'They're all very much alike. I'll take one, haphazard,' he declares before delivering the miraculous capability to the eponymous fellow, a Mr. Fotheringay, who is just about to order a pint at his local bar.

In our reimagining, the heavenly benefactor would distribute his largesse to a relatively small number of the weak and pitiful creatures who have done practically nothing to deserve his favor, but suddenly find themselves in possession of near-limitless power and influence over the lives of others, if not quite the supernatural capacities of the film's hero. The distribution certainly seems as random, indiscriminate or haphazard as the anthropoid god's selection. Who actually deserves the kind of power enjoyed by celebrities? And I do mean *enjoyed*: while we grow bored of learning of the pressures of being in the public eye, the descent into dependencies on prescription drugs, or booze, the almost obligatory spells in rehab, the struggles with depression, anxiety attacks and other mental illness and the intolerably high expectations that all but force them to undergo repeated plastic surgery, we know that none would dream of swapping life as a celeb for a return to the mundane.

Kim Kardashian has never knowingly complained; she evidently luxuriates in the celebrity lifestyle, availing herself of every conceivable indulgence. She probably hasn't seen the old film or read Wells' sci-fi classic, but she must surely feel a bit like Mr. Fotheringay, who discovers to his astonishment that he can wreak brutal retribution on a police officer who upsets him (sends him to Hell) or even stop the world from spinning. Deeds that are literally impossible become doable at a stroke.

Of course, Fotheringay has no idea what he's done to deserve his superpowers and, though he ruminates about it, the source of them remains mysterious. The source of Kim's superpowers is less arcane, but only slightly less. After all, like Fotheringay, she hasn't actually done anything exceptional, at least nothing so exceptional that it warrants being blessed.

It can appear as if Kim has been favored, like Fotheringay, by the gods. But she has worked cleverly and maybe industriously at attracting the kind of attention from the media that only the likes of Madonna and, before her, Elizabeth Taylor, commanded. Of course, this pair was reliant on traditional media (apologies to Madonna, who is still around and still getting plenty of media attention, but, as we'll discover in Chapter 2, her particular skill was in mesmerizing press and broadcast media). Kim was able to take advantage of Web 2.0, this being the second stage of the development of the internet which allowed user-generated content and the growth of social media — as opposed to the static web pages that appeared before 2005 (the innovation was launched in December 2004 and expanded over the next several years).

A version of celebrity culture had emerged before the interactive internet, of course. Our preoccupation with people who made no material impact on our lives and who had distinguished themselves only by appearing so many times in the media that we felt we knew them preceded Web 2.0 by many years. Yet there was something like a cultural somersault after about 2005 and our fascination turned.

Instead of reading about, looking at and exchanging opinions about people who, for some reason, interested us, we could engage with them. *Engage* is one of the words of our age. Everyone seems to use it and we think they know what it means, even in the absence of a definition. I'll define it as attracting or occupying someone's interest or attention in a way that leads to establishing what seems meaningful contact or connection. It sounds unnecessarily wordy, but I don't want to stand accused of vagueness on what is, after all, a crucial term. It's more than just feeling involved in someone else's life; fans from the 1950s to the 1990s no doubt experienced this kind of involvement. Today, they feel they can touch and be touched, and share thoughts reciprocally.

Somersault is probably not the best metaphor, actually: the new technology gave celebrity followers the means to turn their relationships inside out. They no longer stood on the outside looking in. Kim Kardashian was among the first of a new generation of prospective celebs who were prepared to spread out the welcome mat. It's easy to see why Kardashian was so popular. She didn't just invite people into her world, or at least what passed convincingly as her world. She provided them with close-up pictures for posterity. The close-ups might have actually been too close, but the content was high-order trivia. And, somehow, the insignificance of Kim and her messages conferred a delectable immediacy. Perfect for the noughties, when audiences had become accustomed to a kind of intimacy.

The discrepancy between the old-school Hollywood public image and real person, had been closed up over the last two decades of the twentieth century. But popular culture never stands still for long, and social media, particularly twitter, which launched in 2006, provided a new kind of grammar. It was an odd, but original structure of communication and it enabled fans to talk – after a fashion – with the objects of their attention.

Kim and her relatives brought fans within whispering distance. They allowed millions to share their personal agony, despair, euphoria and transports of delight. Think back, if you can, to 2003, the year of the Streisand case. Eminem, Pink, *Pirates of the Caribbean: The Curse of the Black Pearl*,

DVDs, Lance Armstrong wins his fifth Tour de France. Someone approaches you and invites you to invest in a computer-based operation that allows people to exchange information with each other, but only in 140-character messages. Do you want to pump your life savings into it? Twitter is worth about $22 billion today.

Kim and the other Kardashians' association with social media is a story that goes in an unexpected direction. Several unexpected directions, really. Kim herself, as everyone knows, became probably the most influential figure on the net: she had 110 million followers on Instagram and commanded $500,000 (£385,000) per post, slightly less than Selena Gomez, with whom she vied for top influencer (more on this in Chapter 5). Kardashian sisters – Kendall and Kylie Jenner – boasted 82 million and 95 million followers each.

Brother Rob Kardashian was slapped with a restraining order after posting explicit images of his ex Blac Chyna online. A model and former stripper; he'd leaked naked pictures of her on Instagram (a criminal offense in California). Sister Khloé became the queen of all things fitness and weight loss thanks to her app *Khloé With A K*. Half-sister Kendall Jenner – the world's highest paid model with yearly earnings of over $22 million – had one of her YouTube ads pulled by Pepsi after criticism that it appeared to trivialize demonstrations aimed at tackling social justice causes. Kylie, a self-styled makeup maven made parents gasp when she boasted that her daughter Stormi's footwear collection was worth $22,000; the child was four months old at the time. Kylie was also reported to be the world's youngest self-made billionaire in March 2019 (I'll explain how she made it in Chapter 8).

In one way or another, the family has managed to dominate social media. Not in the way Romans dominated parts of Britain, or in the way the Protestant work ethic still pervades large parts of the world. But in the way the Statue of Liberty dominates the New York skyline or the Burj Khalifa dwarfs all other buildings in Dubai. The Kardashians wielded power and influence through social media. The reason why they have been able to march on imperiously is that the social media themselves, or itself (to be ungrammatical but current), is part of everyone's lives. And before doubters protest, I should explain that even those who loathe and avoid social media are, whether they like it or not, implicated in it.

The Kardashians have dragged celebrity culture into its second era – the social media period. For many, this means that the once-humble social networking website called the Facebook (they dropped the 'the' in 2005) was a benediction digitally bonded to a curse. What started as a means through which people with common interests could chat and swap pictures together became the Kardashians route to world domination. Like a pet gecko that grows into Godzilla.

Thanks to the Kardashians and you, readers, the first casualties of the digital age are rationality, logic and common sense; there is no apparent rhyme or reason to our captivation with people who appear, observe, respond and react with silent thoughts. That's pretty much it. It was a clever idea to feature a woman and her family in a show about nothing-in-particular. Now, the idea has been expanded so far that it's changed everything. We follow the Kardashians and other celebrities like hungry animals scavenging for nutritious scraps. Call it perverse. Call it dystopic. But our pursuit of them has changed everything: our understanding of gender, sex, race, consumption, privacy, fame and even ourselves. Not convinced? Read on. There are chapters on all these.

(There is, of course, only one proper way to tell a story: start at the middle, then zigzag all the way to the past by way of the present. I realize the readers might occasionally feel like passengers on an overnight train, waking to look out of the window and wondering, 'Where are we now?' To appease the linear-minded among you, I've compiled a time-line of the key events that appear in these pages, which you've probably already glanced at. Use it as a time-ordering reference when the zigzagging makes you feel queasy.)

TIMELINE

1899
Economist Thorstein Veblen (1857–1929) introduces the term *conspicuous consumption* to describe expenditure on products and services bought to enhance one's prestige rather than for their practical utility.

1909
Harry Selfridge (1858–1947) opens a store in London; it has 100 departments and restaurants and is designed to make shopping an enjoyable experience rather than a functional necessity.

1920
Herbert Hoover (1874–1964) is elected US President and encourages stabilization of wages, higher profits and lower retail prices for goods, resulting in the beginnings of consumer society; he presides until 1933, when Franklin D. Roosevelt takes office and introduces his New Deal, a massive public works program to reduce unemployment during the Great Depression.

1938
Robert K. Merton publishes an influential monograph in which he explains how America encourages aspirational consumption of consumer products.

1943
Abraham Maslow (1908–70) publishes an influential psychological paper on motivation, in which he introduces the term *self-actualization,* meaning the realization or fulfillment of one's talents and potentialities; this will be promoted by successive generations.

1957
The Hidden Persuaders, a book by Vance Packard (1914–96), reveals how advertising draws on motivational research to manipulate and influence consumers' buying habits, often using subliminal suggestion, i.e. below the threshold of sensation or consciousness, so that consumers remain unaware.

1962

Marcello Geppetti (1933–98), a paparazzo, takes photographs of an unsuspecting Elizabeth Taylor trysting with Richard Burton on Ischia, an island in the Tyrrhenian Sea; the images start a major scandal and pique public interest in the private lives of Hollywood stars.

1965

An uprising in the Watts district of LA has a contagious effect and, for the next two years, there is rioting across the USA, blacks protesting against racism.

1966

The Black Panthers, an influential black militant organization, emerges in Oakland, California.

1968

James Brown (1933–2006) releases *Say It Loud – I'm Black and I'm Proud*

1969

Stonewall riots in New York's Greenwich Village reveal militancy among gay people. (Later, in 2019, New York's police commissioner, James O'Neill, apologizes, "the actions taken by the NYPD were wrong.")

1970

Kent State University, in Ohio, is the scene of a student protest against the USA's invasion of Cambodia; members of the Ohio National Guard respond by firing into a crowd, killing four and wounding nine unarmed students. The event symbolizes the divisions that split the nation over the Vietnam War.

1975

Arnold Schwarzenegger wins the Mr Olympia title for a sixth year in a row. (he has won global bodybuilding competitions at least once a year for the previous 10 years), and sets himself a new goal: to be the most popular actor in the world; in 1984, he will play a cyborg assassin in James Cameron's movie *The Terminator*.

1976

Elton John reveals to *Rolling Stone* that he is bisexual.
Bruce Jenner wins Olympic gold in the decathlon.
A journalist reveals that the winner of the women's championship at a tennis tournament, Renée Clark aka Renée Richards, has previously competed as a man; earlier, in 1952, Christine Jorgensen famously became USA's first person to undergo sex reassignment surgery.

1977

George Benson's hit *The Greatest Love of All* contains the lines,"Learning to love yourself/It is the greatest love of all."

1979

The Culture of Narcissism by Christopher Lasch is published; the author analyzes a society in which, "to live for the moment is the prevailing passion – to live for yourself, not for your predecessors or posterity."

1980

Kim Kardashian is born.
Narcissistic personality disorder is included in the third edition of the *Diagnostic and Statistical Manual of Mental Disorder (DSM-III)* published by American Psychiatric Association.
American Gigolo is released and effectively launches the Armani label.

1981

Jane Fonda's *Workout Book* is published; it will be followed in a year by a companion video.
MTV is launched; its programs consist of music videos.

1982

Jean-Paul Goude's book *Jungle Fever* is published. Victoria's Secret is bought by The Limited: outlets appear in shopping malls.

1984

Elton John marries Renate Blauel, a woman; the marriage will last four years.

1989

Madonna's video for *Like a Prayer* is condemned by the Vatican. Pepsi pull an advertising campaign featuring extracts from the video, which includes images of burning crosses, stigmata and a saint's icon made flesh.

1990

Madonna's Blond Ambition World Tour.
Madonna's video for *Justify My Love* features her being seduced by a mysteriously androgynous figure played by supermodel Amanda Cazalet, who later claims Madonna "stalked" her for two years after the filming.

1991

Madonna: Truth or Dare (aka *In Bed with Madonna*) is released. She says: "I think everybody has a bisexual nature". *The Jerry Springer Show* launches. Bruce Jenner marries Kris Kardashian (April 21).

1992

MTV launches *The Real World*; from 2013, it will be *Real World*.
Whitney Houston marries Bobby Brown amid rumors of her lesbian romance.
Anna Nicole Smith appears twice in *Playboy*; once on the front cover, once in centerfold.

1994

Smith, 26, marries 89-year-old billionaire J. Howard Marshall II and declares: "I love the paparazzi. They take pictures and I just smile away. I've always liked attention."

1995

A sex tape featuring Pamela Anderson and her husband Tommy Lee is released.
Gianni Versace comes out in an interview with *The Advocate*.
Casio launch the QV-10 digital (i.e. film-free) camera (see also 2002).

1996

Anna Nicole Smith files for bankruptcy a year after husband J. Howard Marshall II dies.
Madonna, now 38, gives birth to daughter Lourdes.

1997

Versace is murdered on the steps of his mansion at Miami's South Beach.
Aged 50, Elton John appears at the funeral of Diana, Princess of Wales with his partner David Furnish.
Arnold Schwarzenegger appears nude in *Cosmopolitan*.

1998

George Michael is arrested for committing "lewd acts" in Beverly Hills.

2000

Paris Hilton signs as a model with T Models, Donald Trump's modeling agency.
Kim Kardashian marries music producer Damon Thomas; they will divorce in 2004.
US version of *Big Brother* premieres.

2002

The Anna Nicole Show launches on E!
The Sanyo SCP-5300 clamshell style phone incorporates a camera, innovating on technology launched in Japan two years before; by the end of 2003, 80 million camera-phones will have been sold globally.
Christina Aguilera's *Beautiful* contains the line, "I am beautiful in every single way."

2003

A tape featuring Paris Hilton engaged in sex with Rick Salomon (two years before), and which becomes known as *1 Night in Paris*, is released on the internet; 15 years later, Hilton describes the experience: "It was like being raped."
The Simple Life starts on Fox TV, later transferring to E! It features Paris Hilton and Nicole Richie – both wealthy socialites – doing menial jobs, such as cleaning, farm work and serving fast food; the show will run for five seasons; the first episode is screened the week after Hilton's sex tape is released.
Arnold Schwarzenegger is elected Governor of California; shortly before the election, he is accused of sexual harassment.
Barbra Streisand's attempt to suppress photographs taken of her house by legal means backfires and attracts so much publicity that online viewers visit the site on which the images of her home are published. The paradox of producing great publicity from an attempt to quell it becomes known as the Streisand Effect. The case signals the inability of celebrities, no matter how well known, respected or admired, to subdue the media and the interest it can prompt in audiences.
Robert Kardashian dies of cancer.

2004

Paris Hilton's book *Confessions of an Heiress* becomes a bestseller.
Hilton introduces her first fragrance in association with Parlux; by 2017, she will have 24 fragrances in the range; she appoints Kim Kardashian as her personal stylist.
Web 2.0 allows interactivity online; Facebook is founded.

2005

The film *House of Wax* featuring Paris Hilton is released.
Hilton debuts as a DJ at the São Paulo Pop Music Festival; she continues to DJ, commanding seven-figure fees around the world.
Kanye West says, "George Bush doesn't care about black people" during a charity telethon for Hurricane Katrina's victims.
YouTube launches.

2006

Tarana Burke, an African American civil rights activist coins the phrase 'Me Too' as a rallying slogan to publicize awareness of the pervasive sexual abuse; in 2017, the phrase will be prefixed with # and used as an online version of Burke's endeavor.
Paris Hilton releases an album *Paris*.
Kim Kardashian appears fleetingly in episodes of *The Simple Life*.
Kim, Kourtney and Khloé Kardashian open a boutique called D-A-S-H; they will open other outlets, but the business will fold in 2018.

2007

A tape featuring Kim Kardashian and rapper Ray J. having sex is released online via TMZ (February).

Anna Nicole Smith dies from an accidental overdose (February).

Twitter begins a rapid growth; the first ever hashtag is posted; it is #barcamp (March).

Paris Hilton is sentenced to 45 days in jail for a probation violation (April).

Kim Kardashian agrees to a reputed $5 million settlement after suing for invasion of privacy (May).

Apple introduces the iPhone, a device that allows watching films, listening to music and browsing the internet as well as having a 2 mega-pixel camera; by 2017, 1.2 trillion digital photographs per year will be taken, 85 percent on smartphones (June).

Keeping Up With the Kardashians launches to poor reviews on E! (October). There will be several spinoff shows, including *Kourtney and Khloé Take Miami* (2009) and *Rob & Chyna* (2016).

Kim, age, 27, appears naked on the cover of *Playboy* (December).

2008

Paris Hilton returns to television with *Paris Hilton's My New BFF*; two international spinoffs will launch over the next year.

L'Oréal is accused of whitening Beyoncé's skin in cosmetics ads.

2009

Kanye West interrupts VMAs as Taylor Swift is accepting her award. "I'll let you finish, but Beyoncé has one of the best videos of all time," he tells Swift.

Kim Kardashian joins twitter.

Jersey Shore starts on MTV.

2010

Shortly after his death in June, police find skin lightening creams at the home of Michael Jackson, who was long believed to have had skin condition vitiligo that creates patches of de-pigmented skin.

Kim Kardashian launches the first of her line of fragrances.

2011

Halle Berry says of her daughter, "I feel she's black. I'm black and I'm her mother, and I believe in the one-drop theory," in the midst of a custody dispute.

Kim Kardashian marries Kris Humphries in front of 400 guests and E! cameras; she will file for divorce in 72 days.

2012

Whitney Houston dies. The L.A. County Coroner's office gives the cause of death as "drowning and effects of atherosclerotic heart disease and cocaine use."

Kim Kardashian starts seeing musician Kanye West. Trayvon Martin, a 17-year-old African American, is shot and killed by George Zimmerman, a neighborhood watch volunteer; Zimmerman will be acquitted, leading to the rise of #BlackLivesMatter (see below, 2013).

2013

#BlackLivesMatter launches in response to the violence against black people.
Kris Kardashian and Bruce Jenner announce their separation (October 8),
citing irreconcilable differences.
Kanye West signs an endorsement contract with adidas; in February 2015, adidas
will launch West's Yeezy line of footwear; in May 2018, adidas will be under pressure
to drop West after his remarks on slavery (see 2018, below).
'Selfie' is named word of the year by Oxford Dictionaries after the frequency
of its usage increased by 17,000% over the previous 12 months;
Disney's *Frozen* "destabilizes the heteronormative gender roles and conventions that
Disney has circulated in most of its animated fairy-tale films since 1937," as
American Studies professor Heike Steinhoff puts it; the film goes on to become one
of the highest grossing films ever.

2014

Kris files for divorce from Bruce (September 22), which is finalized in less
than three months. Bruce Jenner celebrates his 65th birthday (October 28).
Laverne Cox, transgender star of *Orange is the New Black*, appears on the cover
of *Time*. Kim Kardashian marries Kanye West; the wedding is in Florence.
Kim pastiches Jean-Paul Goude's images from 1982 (see above).
The mobile game, *Kim Kardashian: Hollywood*, brings in over $43million in sales
during the first three months after its launch (June).

2015

 Kylie Jenner, at 17, posts Instagrams showing her with plump pouting lips, setting
off social media discussions about whether she has undergone surgery or lip
augmentation; the "Kylie Jenner Lip Challenge" in which young women insert their
lips into a shot glass, then suck out the air, goes viral; in 2015, Kyle will admit to
having temporary lip fillers; in 2018, *Forbes* will report, "she's conservatively worth
$900 million." ABC television screens *20/20* special two-hour interview with Diane
Sawyer and Caitlyn Jenner, who has completed her transition by the time the show
aired (April 24).
Vanity Fair features pictures of Jenner and the caption "Call Me Caitlyn" on the cover
of its July edition.
Germaine Greer issues an opinion on trans women: "Just because you lop off your
dick and then wear a dress doesn't make you a fucking woman."
Rachel Dolezal resigns from her position at the NAACP after widespread criticism
following her parents' declaration that she is white.
Apple releases Kim Kardashian's emoji pack for iOS. Kim also publishes her first
book *Selfish*, which contains 325 selfies is her.

2016

George Michael dies of natural causes aged 53. Colin Kaepernick, a football player, refuses to stand while the American national anthem plays before the start of an NFL game in protest at the number of blacks slain at the hands of police. In 2018 Kaepernick will receive the Amnesty International Ambassador of Conscience Award.

2017

Kim Kardashian is accused of having her facial skin darkened specifically for a photoshoot, in which she is called "America's New First Lady" and is dressed in a style resembling that of Jackie Onassis; she announces a children's clothing range called TheKidsSupply; she launches KKW, a line of cosmetics.
Forbes magazine names Kendall Jenner the world's highest paid model; she earns $22 million in 2017.
Bill Cosby stands trial for sexual abuse; the jury deliberates for five and half days before declaring itself unable to reach a verdict (June).
New York Times runs a story that alleges Harvey Weinstein has sexually abused women.
Alyssa Milano launches #MeToo, an online campaign designed to encourage women to share their experiences of sexual abuse; it will be used 12 million times over the next three months and continues to be used. Milano is not aware of Tarana Burke's earlier use of the phrase (see 2006, above).

2018

Bill Cosby is convicted of drugging and molesting an acquaintance (April); since the mistrial ten months earlier (see above), the #MeToo movement has emerged. Journalist Hadley Freeman echoes the view of doubters when she writes: "It looks like #MeToo didn't topple the patriarchy – it showed how tenacious the patriarchy is at enforcing its stranglehold."
Kanye West says: "When you hear about slavery for 400 years ... for 400 years? That sounds like a choice," during a TMZ newsroom conversation. He adds: "We're mentally in prison." He also makes headlines by declaring support for President Donald Trump.
A team of psychologists coins the word "selfitis" to describe the obsessive taking of selfies.
A man breaks into Taylor Swift's New York townhouse, takes a shower before being arrested while sleeping in her bed.
Later in the year, Kim and Khloé are criticized for joking about anorexia.
Kylie Jenner ($1 million per post) and Selena Gomez ($800,000 per post) are reported to be the highest paid celebrities on Instagram.
Kim Kardashian, in a paid post, urges her 111 million followers to try appetite-suppressing lollipops; after protest, she deletes the post; sister Khloé, in another paid post, advises replacing a meal per day with an appetite suppressing milkshake to lose baby weight. Both women come under criticism for not including health warnings in their posts.

2019

Kim Kardashian issues an apology after being accused of 'cultural appropriation' with her new shapewear venture and promises to change the brand name "Kimono."

CHAPTER 2

EMASCULATED WOMANHOOD

In view of the number of movies about curses that can be passed on simply by watching a video – watch this and you'll receive visits from the undead (*The Curse*); watch another and die within seven days (*The Ring*); or see how you like this and turn into a zombie (*The Evil Dead*) – it's a wonder no one has come up with a diabolical plot about Madonna's *Madonna: Truth or Dare* (or *In Bed with Madonna*, as it was called in some parts of the world). Sit still for a couple of hours watching a videotape of this 1991 film (they used videocassettes back then), which is a kind of feature-length precursor of what we now call reality TV, and you'll turn into an inveterate voyeur and spend the rest of your days as a restless, tormented spirit wandering through the arid wastelands of other people's lives. As in the curse films, seemingly harmless entertainment instigates alterations in our mood, temperament, taste and habits. All for the worse.

We'll never know how Madonna came into possession of her unholy power, though you'd sometimes swear that, on the cusp of the 1990s, someone vested her with a crystal ball and bade her to stare deeply until she saw the future. That future was one in which the division between the private and

21

the public lives of popular entertainers would disappear and anyone with their sights set on stardom would need to make a Mephistophelean deal: a private life in exchange for all the adulation the world can provide. Madonna took a deep breath of sulphur and surrendered what might have been, in other eras, a personal life.

The film was ostensibly a documentary chronicling Madonna's Blond Ambition tour of 1990; among her many stage costumes was a now-iconic pink cone bra bustier. The senses of the audience were sharpened by the candidness of the film; it counterbalanced the extravagant theater of the onstage performance with dressing room conversations and sniping, so that the viewers felt like peeping toms, but without any pang of guilt. Madonna had been thriving on the very thing that had in the past killed off stars: scandal.

Only one Hollywood star had successfully exploited scandal to her own advantage. Elizabeth Taylor was barracked, vilified and spat at after an affair with her late ex-husband's best friend. Fortified rather than humbled by the pillorying, she married Eddie Fisher; then, with her typical capricious éclat, she started another, this time, unpardonable affair with Richard Burton. Far from ruining her, the Burton affair took her to the rarefied heights of celebritydom. For nearly two decades from 1962 (when her relationship with Burton began), Taylor prevailed superiorly, her every move documented by the media and followed by audiences.

Taylor didn't ask for her life to be read as a lesson in how-to-break-rules-and-succeed; but that's how Madonna might have interpreted it. Twenty-one years after the Taylor–Burton scandal broke, Madonna released her first album and started a show business career that could have been designed to shock and offend. A standard-bearer for self-reliant womanhood, Madonna ardently upset as many people as possible, while rising transcendentally to her status as the rightful successor to Taylor.

At a time when men governed, sometimes domineered, and, so we learned later, occasionally tyrannized women, Madonna refused to plot any course to the top other than in her own haphazard way. Yet there was a method in her apparent randomness. She'd divined the future perfectly and saw a world in which, to succeed, stars, or celebrities as they were to become, had to sacrifice their private lives, opening themselves up to inspection by a gossip-hungry public, and in which scandal, far from being an improvised explosive device that could devastate a showbiz career, was a valuable resource. Paris Hilton and later, Kim Kardashian could attest to that. If Madonna stood on Taylor's Chanel shoulder pads, Hilton and Kardashian stood on her Gaultiers.

'Madonna is the future of feminism,' wrote Camille Paglia in the *New York Times* in late 1990. Not only 'an international star of staggering dimensions. She is also a shrewd business tycoon, a modern woman of all-around talent.' Paglia, then a professor at Philadelphia's University of the Arts, was what you might call a contrarian; she opposed or rejected popular feminists' perspectives, while remaining a stalwart supporter of independent-minded femininity. She'd been unsparing in exposing what she thought were the hypocrisies of feminists who 'want men to be like women.' But, in Madonna, Paglia saw someone who had 'a far profounder vision of sex than do the feminists. She sees both the animality and the artifice.'

Madonna's taboo-breaking might have been staged and have too much intention to be considered anything but a theatrical stratagem. Then again, she didn't appear, or expect any of her fans to feel virtuous. Paglia regarded her performance as a demonstration to young women how to be 'attractive, sensual, energetic, ambitious, aggressive and funny.'

Madonna might have used Paglia's validation as encouragement for further animalism (that is, behavior, especially physical, that's characteristic of animals). No other book published in 1992 received as much publicity as *Sex*, a sheet metal-covered book of photographs featuring Madonna in poses that suggested lesbianism, anal sex and sadomasochism. Its publication coincided with the release of *Erotica*, an album that complemented the book thematically. The accompanying video featured Madonna, then 33, dressed androgynously. This was a star at or approaching the peak of her global notoriety, fabulously rich with several hugely successful albums and a presence in movies baring herself and playing out sexual fantasies with anyone who cared to look.

For what? Mischief? Outrage and media exposure were umbilical. Madonna's intuitive brilliance in both brought rewards in the shape of a seven-year $60 million deal with Time-Warner. Around this time, softish porn material from her background began to emerge, so her stylized bawdiness functioned as a distraction from this. By then, Madonna was like a dentist who once drilled teeth without anesthetic and whose patients were now getting used it.

The term postfeminism wasn't invented for Madonna. But it could have been. If people were searching for a phrase to capture the challenge to the traditional version of feminism – the version that took its cues from Simone De Beauvoir's *The Second Sex*, first published in 1949 – today, they would have probably gone for alt-feminism. In the early 1990s, everything stimulating or provocative was prefixed with *post* (as in -modern, -colonial, -Fordism, -punk). Madonna emerged as a personification of postfeminism.

'The female celebrity embodies a presentation of knowingness and confidence, as one who is entrepreneurial in her performance of sexiness, and that offers the possibility for new

formulations and alternative figurations of female sexuality,'
wrote Adrienne Evans, a media scholar and Sarah Riley, a
psychologist, in their 2013 article 'Immaculate Consumption:
Negotiating the Sex Symbol in Postfeminist Culture.' They
wrote of the 'postfeminist masquerade of celebrity' that pro-
duces in young women feelings of failure and 'inability to
engage in the constant beauty and sexiness regimes of
celebrity.'

The postfeminist, in this view, is possessed of a spirit of
independence, though it's an entrepreneurial rather than
recalcitrant or rebellious spirit. Among the resources she
trades is her sexiness. Note: not sex, but sexiness, which is
the quality of being sexually attractive or exciting. Evans and
Riley believe postfeminist celebs perform a kind of sexiness
that, over the years, has become a kind of standard to which
a generation aspires.

You could argue that Madonna proved that the best way
to honor femininity is to strip it naked. Only then will it be
clear that, as Angela McRobbie advised in a 2008 article,
'There is no original, or natural, femininity, it is always a
kind of staging.'

'*Cosmopolitan* places women's value primarily on their ability to sexually satisfy a man and therefore plays into the same
culture where men view and treat women as inanimate sex
objects.' The statement came from the National Center on
Sexual Exploitation, a US organization that campaigns
against pornography, and which had been working with the
retail chain Walmart (owner of British Asda supermarkets) to
remove the international magazine, a scion of the Hearst
Media empire, from the shelves of its 5000 stores.
Cosmopolitan had been in existence since the nineteenth century, but spirited by the zeitgeist of the 1960s, reconfigured
under the editorship of Helen Gurley Brown as a publication

that reflected the strengthening independence of women as career-pursuing controllers of their own destinies with enough confidence to talk and read about sexuality – from a female perspective.

Gurley Brown's best-selling book *Sex and the Single Girl* was published in 1962 and encouraged women to seek physical gratification as well as a professional career. Its idea was to discuss sex without guilt and, for that matter, without the prurience typically associated with the subject. This was 1962, remember, the year before the publication of Betty Friedan's *The Feminine Mystique* and eight years before Germaine Greer's *The Female Eunuch* was published. 'Fun, fearless advice on men, love and sex,' is how *Cosmopolitan*'s website described its remit nearly a half-century later.

In March 2018, Walmart decided that its customers could find *Cosmopolitan* in the magazine section of its stores, but that it would no longer be available by the checkout aisles. In a Facebook live video, the Walmart group's vice president of advocacy and outreach Haley Halverson said:

> *This is one less drop of hyper-sexualized media that is going to be bombarding people in their everyday lives, which does make a difference, especially in this Me Too culture that we're living in, where we really want a culture that will respect women and ensure their dignity is understood.*

Some, including *Healthcare* columnist Dr. Eugene Gu disagreed; she tweeted: 'Removing *Cosmopolitan* magazine from checkout lines at the behest of a Republican censorship organization that hates female sexuality is not a victory for the #MeToo movement. It's a severe perversion of it.' (I will move on to #MeToo later in this chapter.)

The dispute was about what happens to our moral ground after the equivalent of a tsunami has disturbed, overwhelmed and left us quaking; for a moment, we couldn't think straight. Was Walmart behaving in a way consistent with the post-Weinstein sensibilities? After all, it was sparing its customers a discourse over and beyond the normal — whatever that is — accounts of human sexuality. That's presumably what Halverson meant when she referred to the hyper-sexualized media (*hyper* usually means above and beyond 'normal'). Or was it conflating and confusing voyeurism with serious, informed, if intemperate, usually epicurean and, occasionally, licentious discussion? Kim Kardashian didn't have a ready answer, though she could probably have come up with something if she felt inclined to refer back eleven years to an episode in her own life.

The story of *Kim Kardashian, Superstar*, a 41-minute video released by Vivid Entertainment in 2007 was a news sensation. It would have been too fantastic to believe if her former employer Paris Hilton hadn't featured in something similar three years before. That was punningly titled *1 Night in Paris*. The then 23-year-old Hilton Hotels heiress was worth at least a couple of hundred million and had no need for a cheap publicity stunt. All the same, it made her seriously famous. So it seemed like a royal succession when Kardashian assumed the throne as queen of scandal.

'This tape which ... was meant to be something private between myself and my then-boyfriend [Ray J., a rapper] is extremely hurtful not only to me, but to my family as well,' Kardashian told Lorenzo Benet of *People* magazine in 2007 (February 21). 'I am filing legal charges against the company who is distributing this tape since it is being sold completely without my permission or consent.'

This hardly sounded like auspicious start to the career of someone who would, within a few years, pronounce:

*For me, [a] feminist is someone who advocates for
the civil and social rights and liberties of all people,
regardless of their gender; anyone who believes that
women should have the same choices and
opportunities as men when it comes to education
and employment, their bodies and their lifestyles ....
Of course I want these things! I'm all about
empowering and uplifting women.*

This is what Kardashian wrote in an essay for her website in
August 2016. She and Hilton were far from the only women
who had featured in sex tapes. Pamela Anderson and
Jennifer Lopez were among others. But Kardashian and
Hilton were the two who profited most from the global
exposure that followed and, of course, this was made possible by the internet.

To her many detractors there will be little or nothing in
this book to change their minds and see Kardashian as anything other than a paragon of blandness; she offers nothing
that's stimulating, spirited or remotely challenging to the
kind of sexist culture that has persisted for decades; she is
vapid and superficial, bloodless and trite. I tend to think differently, but not because I see Kardashian and indeed her
family differently. Kardashian is no feminist leader, nor even
a self-conscious feminist for that matter but she is arguably
emblematic of the disruptions in production and consumption that have taken place over the past decade on a meaningful, perhaps revolutionary scale. And these changes centrally
involve women.

It's not just women's bodies that are on the market; almost
nothing lies outside the celebrity market's ability to package,
monetize and, as I'll argue in Chapter 8, leverage. But why
treat the market as an abstract force when we can identify so
many women whose marketization – exposing themselves

for sale to an audience of potential buyers – is a self-willed deed? Is it exploitation if made possible by grace and freewill?

———————————

Emily Ratajkowski is an outspoken feminist – that's how she describes herself – 'whether addressing body-image issues on Lena Dunham's site, Lenny, or challenging the haters with a topless, in-your-face Instagram alongside Kim Kardashian' as Naomi Wolf puts it. (Lenny Letter was a weekly feminist newsletter created by Dunham, one of the co-creators of *Girls*.) Wolf, in 2016, likened meeting Ratajkowski to meeting the zeitgeist (that word again!) Coming from someone who herself seemed to have captured the spirit of the 1990s between the covers of her book *The Beauty Myth: How Images of Beauty Are Used Against Women* (first published in 1990), this was a quite a commendation.

Writing for the magazine *Harper's Bazaar*, Wolf reflected on Ratajkowski: 'Her views reflect a dramatic shift in the culture, as many young women actually do call themselves feminists these days.' Is Ratajkowski's version, or perhaps reimagining, of feminism the future? Is it even today? The meeting between these two cultural weathervanes provides a point of relative stability while we are caught up in the Weinstein-induced flood of perspectives that change shape and focus almost daily. (I'll get to Weinstein shortly.)

'Because of third-wave feminism, I understood that there are all these fucked-up ideals of beauty put on young women,' declared Ratajkowski, her suggestion being that, following the Friedan/Greer wave of feminism in the 1960s and 1970s, there followed another occurrence or disturbance of the established order around the start of the 1990s and this introduced a more aggressively individualist form of feminism. It implicated women in a project that was, in several senses, their own personal project – as opposed to that of all

women. While earlier waves of feminism, or women's liberation, as it was often called, fought for the liberation of
women from all manner of inequalities and their subservient
status in relation to men, as well as against the hidebound
attitudes causing them, the next wave presented women with
a more manageable reality: improve yourselves as individuals
and other women will be inspired to emulate you.

Part of the project involved understanding and critiquing
the media, which, by the mid-1990s, was globalizing in a
way that would turn it into the indomitable force it now is.
The words we used, thoughts we entertained and visions we
conjured were all, in some measure, affected by the media
and third-wave feminism criticized the casual, often careless
but also frequently injurious language we used without reflection. Words didn't just reflect but shaped ideas on womanhood, gender, sexuality, femininity, masculinity and, well,
practically anything, including beauty. This was, in part,
Wolf's assignment in her 1990 book: she wanted to expand
on earlier feminist arguments to show how a 'cultural conspiracy' had served to make women constantly feel inad-
equate because they didn't have the physical attributes that
measured up to a particular standard of beauty.

Women, argued Wolf, had been fed the notion that to be
beautiful they would have to conform to a particular 'look'.
They should be as thin as the near-anorexic models that
populated fashion pages, have a youthful, blemish-free skin
and hair that would shame Rapunzel. This checklist was
intimidating to most women and either sapped their confidence or turned them into avid shoppers of cosmetics, groom-
ing products and services that promised eternal youth (plastic
surgery being the best-promoted and commercially successful
one). The media's power was not then at its peak; there was
no internet. But it played a pivotal part in dispensing the

widely held but false belief that women could attain the ideal, the beauty myth.

'Gaslighting' is the term sometimes used to describe a surreptitious manipulation of women into doubting their own worth. The word comes from the 1944 movie *Gaslight*, in which a man psychologically maneuvers his wife, played by Ingrid Bergman, into believing she's going insane. While Wolf didn't mention the word, the process she described resembles a social equivalent of gaslighting.

Wolf's book was both a sardonic comment and condemnation of an unpleasant world in which women were serially, sexually exploited, imbued with self-doubt and driven to pathological extremes in their futile pursuit of an impossible dream. But from this, something else emerges: a socially aware and knowing generation of women who knew all about the conniving monsters who perpetrated the myth, either on purpose or by default, but had grown comfortable being implicated in a conspiracy they had seen through and, actually, didn't find as objectionable as outsiders might suppose. That's the thing about conspiracies: even when the plan is exposed, there are often people who have been so taken in that they can't envision alternatives.

By 2016, Wolf concluded, 'there's still the fear and contempt of female sexuality and the just intolerable cultural reaction when women take ownership of their sexuality and their bodies.' She invited Ratajkowski to respond:

> *Kim [Kardashian] said that to me. You know, when Lena Dunham takes her clothes off, she gets flack, but it's also considered brave; when Justin Bieber takes his shirt off, he's a grown-up. But when a woman who is sexual takes off her top, it plays into something.*

Wolf's argument was, and presumably is, that Ratajkowski, Kardashian and many other women who have few inhibitions about their bodies and seem to exhibit themselves as if in naked defiance of cultural norms are creating objects around or from their own bodies and asserting their right to circulate these as freely as they wish. Madonna had to make do with theater, film, TV and print. Digitization has made it possible to short-circuit traditional media. It's also made possible an exponential growth of pornography, by which I mean visual material with explicit display (or description: there is pornographic prose) specifically intended to stimulate sexual arousal.

There is a crucial distinction between exhibitionism and pornography and, while Wolf doesn't inspect it, women who parade themselves in a way that might provoke a sexual response, may, however inadvertently, produce pornographic material. The reception rather than the production defines what is or isn't porn. 'Women learn what a sexy woman is from porn or from airbrushed Victoria's Secret models, so I would love a world in which you don't have to look like that to say, "Screw you, I own my sexual body"', submitted Wolf. It seems like a somewhat innocent utopia; but one generation's conservatism is probably the next's radicalism. Once writers opt for an honorable position as idealists, they often find themselves beleaguered by successive generations.

Wolf contended: 'There's a deeply anti-feminist origin of mocking women for seeking attention.' By this, I take it that she means the point at which the ridicule begins is in opposition to feminist ideas. Of course, there's also a profoundly pro-feminist argument that seeking attention by objectifying one's own body is a hostile act against the best interests of women.

You can't engage in history, or be a leader, without some drive for recognition. What I really like is that

*you [Emily Ratajkowski] are adding your words to
the pictures and the images – and doing what you
can to control the message – even though you can't
control everything in the industry.*

This isn't an argument to find favor with everyone, nor is
Ratajkowski's approval: 'Sex is normal. Desire is normal.
Attention is normal, and that's okay.'

So Wolf and Ratajkowski seemed to be tilting against
windmills that look very much like the media ('the industry'),
including its workers, owners and, by implication, consumers
who keep them going. You don't have to be familiar with
Cervantes to know that going up against windmills is rarely a
worthwhile activity, especially when those windmills are, in
reality, pillars of modern society. The industry (let's go with
Wolf's term) is unpleasant, exploitative and antediluvian in
its approach to women; it degrades them to the status of
mere objects by exhibiting images of them in a manner that
may, or may not, be, but usually is, sexually arousing to heterosexual men (and others, we surmise). It also rewards
women who are either prepared to or are enthusiastic about
denuding themselves to some degree in an effort to be, as
Wolf put it, 'engaged in establishing a new narrative to
reclaim the body.'

'Celebrity culture is an arena organised on the threshold
between the public and the private, with privacy a commodity to be accrued, valued and sold,' wrote Sam Riviere, of the
Telegraph, in 2015. 'Extreme self-exposure,' of the kind practiced by Ratajkowski and Kardashian, 'on the one hand
undermines the idea of a person as being detached from their
image, with all the implications of ownership and "fair use"
that that might entail, and on the other involves the projec-
tion of highly mediated public identity, which invites "personal" attention and interaction from viewers and fans.'

Riviere invoked English Literature's favorite sister Virginia Woolf: 'Publicity in women is detestable.' The precept is from *A Room of One's Own*, first published in 1929. 'Kardashian's genuine achievement may be that she has become a singularly successful producer and owner of her own image, and her image alone,' wrote Riviere. Riviere's is an interesting thought: women who self-consciously offer their bodies for display, whether via selfies *à la* Kardashian, or through the lenses of professional photographers, 'do not posit a male viewer as their primary destination.' There is, according to Riviere, an intimacy even in an image shared several million times through Instagram that leaves no room for the prurient distance that characterizes soft porn.

Why should women not want to show off their bodies? What's wrong with desiring the attention of others? Aren't women who flaunt themselves as ostentatiously as they can in order to provoke envy, admiration, defiance and sexual arousal just exercising *agency* – that is, their ability to produce the ends they want? Sober puritans of feminism of yore, as Wolf calls them, would have retorts to all these questions, as would many contemporary feminists. I think of a torture dungeon where captives are taken and shown the various implements of pain, then fed a burger, fries and a latte. 'What's this? My last meal before the thumbscrews go on?' asks a young maiden anticipating the digit-crushing apparatus. To which the torturer replies: 'No, you're free to leave any time you please. But if you decide to stay, we'll keep the food and drink coming. And every so often, we'll expect you to shout out of the barred window that we're treating you well and that you've decided to stay here 'cause the food is good.'

Women are currently enjoying freedoms and protection that were only dreamt of by previous generations; yet their position in the overall structure has not significantly altered:

they're still imprisoned, even if they choose, like those with Stockholm Syndrome, to stick with familiarity rather than gamble with change.

'Casting couch' is an expression with two meanings. The first is literal; it was the piece of furniture on which Hollywood film roles were awarded to female actors in exchange for granting sexual favors to directors, producers or some other man with sway in the industry. The sleazy practice reaches back to the 1940s. 'I've slept with producers, I'd be a liar if I said I didn't,' Marilyn Monroe acknowledged in her 1954 memoir *My Story*, adding that, such was the competition for parts in Hollywood that, 'if you didn't go along, there were 25 girls who would.' The Hollywood exploitation occurred – and perhaps still occurs – behind closed doors and was accepted as a routine part, and not even a regrettable part either, of how business gets done in that part of the world. If anything the phrase carried an unsavoury, comic quality: 'I wonder how she got that part ...?'

The second, metaphorical meaning of 'casting couch' developed into a wider, more venal narrative, not just about Tinseltown, but anywhere in society where men had power and could use it to assist women achieve whatever they desired – the *quid pro quo* was much the same. As film executives imposed their wills on ambitious but powerless women, men in all areas of society would get their own way, using incentives or threats with impunity. With impunity, that is, until life turned grotesque, nightmarish and bizarre for, at first, one man and, later, every man who had used his authority to extort sex from women.

One episode distilled an entire epoch of feminist activism, confrontation and protest over gender equality. Everything changed. On October 5, 2017, the *New York Times* ran a story detailing almost three decades of testimony from women, all accusing the film producer Harvey Weinstein of sexual harassment. It alleged that Weinstein had paid out at least eight settlements. Three days later, he was dismissed from the Weinstein Company, which he had founded in 2005.

It was by no means the first time a powerful man from the entertainment industry had been ruined by a sex scandal. Back in 1921, Roscoe 'Fatty' Arbuckle, then the highest paid actor in the world, was alleged to have raped a struggling wannabe actress named Virginia Rappe. A medical examination showed no evidence of a sexual assault and Arbuckle was eventually cleared, though his reputation was irreparably damaged and he died a destitute smackhead in 1933, aged 46. It was a salutary case and one that prompted the film industry to spin a protective cocoon around its most precious stars, especially its transgressive males. The protection was serviceable; Hollywood and the entertainment industry generally survived the moral strictness of the Production Code era ending 1945, the liberalizing 1960s and beyond. Sex was never far away, of course, and there were claims every so often. But seriously dangerous scandals were hushed up or settled out of court, until Weinstein.

After the *New York Times* story, more women came forward. Rose McGowan and Ashley Judd, both actors, were among the first women to accuse the mogul of sexual misconduct. 'I said "no" a lot of ways, a lot of times,' said Judd. 'Women have been talking about Harvey amongst ourselves for a long time and it's simply beyond time to have the conversation publicly.' Her suggestion was obvious: Weinstein's conduct was well-known in Hollywood and elsewhere.

The New Yorker magazine published a follow-up that alleged 13 more incidents, including three accusations of rape. Why hadn't the women spoken out before? 'He [Weinstein] drags your name through the mud, and he'll come after you hard with his legal team,' a woman told Ronan Farrow for his 2017 article 'From Aggressive Overtures to Sexual Assault: Harvey Weinstein's Accusers Tell Their Stories.' Farrow wrote of 'a culture of silence' that effectively stopped women from making their experiences public; this was, it was claimed, reinforced by nondisclosure agreements which it was alleged Weinstein used as a secret weapon to deter potential accusers. But, a culture of silence is still a culture, meaning that the word of a young woman tends to lack credibility in an environment in which authority is typically attributed to a more powerful, and usually older, and always more powerful man. Then suddenly, the culture of silence seemed to evaporate and in the six months following the exposé something else materialized.

By March 2018, more than 70 women had accused Weinstein of sexual misconduct, including rape, while Weinstein denied having nonconsensual sex with any of them. The movement had been given impetus by an online twitter campaign, #MeToo, that encouraged women in and out of the entertainment industry to share their experiences of abuse and name the men who had violated them. Scores of women came forward identifying themselves as victims; most explained they withheld public disclosure for fear of retribution by powerful movie producers, actors, or public figures from politics and education (and presumably, the fear of being stigmatized). Each new disclosure had the effect of provoking further conjecture, 'how many others?' And the response was, as the hashtag suggests, 'me too.'

The majority of the women who shared their stories were financially and professionally secure. Even those who weren't were able to negotiate deals with the media. They were, by and large, not working at call centers or dishing out fried chicken meals at fast food drive-by windows. Though, of course, there were probably some Weinstein-like characters in these types of working environments. In fact, shortly after the initial disclosures, some 700,000 female farmworkers publicly affirmed their solidarity with their more affluent and celebrated counterparts. 'We believe and stand with you,' the farmworkers stated in an open letter.

A 2016 Equal Employment Opportunity Commission (EEOC) task force report authored by Chai Feldblum and Victoria Lipnic concluded that nearly a third of about 90,000 EEOC employment discrimination charges in 2015 included a workplace harassment allegation; meanwhile, 'much of the training done over the last 30 years has not worked as a pre-vention tool – it's been too focused on simply avoiding legal liability.' And, in the process, protecting the culprits. The report was studiously researched and logically presented, though it didn't have the immediacy of the memes that were hurtling around the world asking questions and provoking minds. For example, the actor Ellen Page used her Facebook page to broaden the field:

> *I have the privilege of having a platform that enables me to write this and have it published, while the most marginalized do not have access to such resources. The reality is, women of color, trans and queer and indigenous women have been leading this fight for decades (forever actually).*

What started as another Hollywood scandal could have lin-gered no longer than it took Weinstein's lawyers to flex their muscles. Writing in the *Los Angeles Times*, Ann Friedman speculated, 'It's dangerously likely that we'll look back five or 10 years from now and realize it was mostly white, wealthy, powerful women who benefited from the aftermath of the Harvey Weinstein allegations' (November 14, 2017). But her fears were unfounded. It seemed like another *he said/*

she said story to begin with; a few months before there had been similar cases involving Andrea Constand who accused Bill Cosby of performing sexual acts on her without consent, and Kesha, who was embroiled in a court battle against producer Dr. Luke, whom she accused of sexual assault and battery, harassment and emotional abuse.

The Weinstein case might have generated less publicity than either of these. After all, Weinstein was known in the entertainment industry and by film aficionados, but not especially beyond. Paradoxically, he had long presented himself as a supporter of women; he'd also been a major donor to Democrat Presidents Barack Obama and Bill Clinton, and was instrumental in endowing a chair at Rutgers University in Gloria Steinem's name. Weinstein's liberal credentials were not in doubt. Perhaps this is the reason why, this time, the world took the claims seriously. It seemed as if the media afforded it more coverage than any event since September 11, 2001. Every day brought a fresh claim and another man shamed, including Kevin Spacey, Dustin Hoffman, Russell Simmons, Louis C.K., and Michael Douglas, amongst others.

Women were daring to suggest that Weinstein, far from being a rogue individual, was actually representative of a larger group of men who were adept at using their power and influence to exact sexual favors. (In Spacey's case, it was a man who made the claim). And they weren't just from the entertainment industry either: there were more from media industries, politics and commerce. Men from different countries, in different industries and at different levels – to put it simply – all men – seemed potential abusers. McGowan, who had accepted $100,000 settlement, which was 'not to be construed as an admission' but 'to avoid litigation and buy peace' tweeted on March 20, 2018, the day after Weinstein's 66th birthday, 'I told you twenty years ago if I heard of you doing this to another girl or woman, we'd come for you.

I would come for you. Happy fucking birthday from all of us. We win.' Women and men had an abrasive, oppressive, exploitative relationship, often based on stereotyping, selfishness and violence. If so, it was worse than the image presented by Friedan and Greer in the 1960s and 1970s.

'Think of your cell phone as your enemy,' a traumatized victim is told by a stalker adviser, instructing her on the perils of social media exposure, in the 2018 Steven Soderbergh movie *Unsane*. But, phones are anything but enemies; in fact, the challenge not simply to Weinstein's alleged serial abuse, but to sexual abuse in the most generic sense, was testament to the power of smartphones, tablets and computers. #MeToo changed the climate. It demonstrated that the reason women had not come forward sooner (the earliest alleged offence committed by Weinstein was against Hope Exiner d'Amore, an employee of his concert promotion company who claimed that Weinstein had raped her in the 1970s) was that they were reluctant to be lone voices. The power of their male abusers was undoubtedly a factor; in Weinstein's case, even suspicious journalists were frustrated by the intimidating pall he cast over women and men alike.

There were reports that Weinstein had tried to suppress Farrow's investigation. But social media faces no such impediments; its beauty is that it creates an effectively lawless milieu in which users are free to share experiences, thoughts, images – memes – and allow them to emerge into cyber consciousness. There are all manner of drawbacks, of course; but let's stay with the colossal benefits reaped by the accusers of at first Weinstein and then several other men. By the end of October 2017 (and the *New York Times* story was October 5), there had been 85 accusers, the most serious claiming Weinstein had raped them, other claiming that he had made sexual advances. This was Weinstein alone.

It is simply unimaginable that such a redoubtable reaction would have been possible without social media. Even the boldest of traditional newspaper editors would have been cautioned by proprietors if they intended to name names. 'Is this a real story, or flight of fancy that's likely to end up in court?' Facebook, Twitter, Instagram and the other digital outlets had no such editorial caveat. If sufficiently emboldened, users could just furnish their accounts with as many details as they cared to share in the knowledge that, once released, their accounts could go viral. McGowan and Judd provided enough material to get matters moving and then, like Frankenstein's creation, the cycle took on a life of its own with women becoming fortified by the legion of others prepared to make allegations and assertions in defiance of legal obstacles.

Weinstein's attorney Charles J. Harder issued a statement about the initial *New York Times* story, which was, he said, defamatory because it relied on 'mostly hearsay accounts.' Of course, hearsay (by which I presume he meant unsubstantiated information) might not be admissible evidence in a court of law, but it has become arguably the most potent force in the digital universe. The censorious comments are usually swatted away like an irritating midge. The force is also, as we all know, a source of weakness: nursery-level stories, negligible ethical codes and mythmaking that seems suspiciously like the wild imaginings of hapless trolls all contribute to a culture in which so-called 'fake news' predominates. But there is so much benefit to be gained in social media that it seems curmudgeonly to detract from its role in effectively introducing what was, in today's vernacular, a game changer.

Prior to 2006, social media was unheard of as a news source. The Facebook newsfeed (which, at first appeared on home pages, and, later, timelines) wasn't intended as an alternative to print media, radio and television. At least not until 2011, when Facebook started displaying news updates on topical stories at the top of the feed. Of course, the cleverness of Facebook was (and is) that it assimilated so much personal information that it could predict the kind of news that would most interest the individual user and tailor the display of stories accordingly. By the time of the Weinstein scandal, Facebook was supported by several other digital conduits that collectively made up not just an adjunct to traditional media, but a formidable rival.

The year 2017 was the first year in history when advertisers spent more on digital media than on television globally, indicating the change in consumers' tastes. Even the most persistent journalists were probably frustrated by their failure to persuade associates or friends of Weinstein and other men to speak on the record. Social media held far fewer hindrances. #MeToo and Time's Up, movements to help victims of sexual harassment with legal defense funding, developed out of social media and continued to draw strength from the self-perpetuating growth of women tired of peer-group persecution and submergence by media.

While it wasn't a conclusive proof of the efficacy of #MeToo, the conviction of Bill Cosby in April 2018 after a mistrial in June 2017 was suggestive of the rapid change in mood. Accused of drugging and sexually assaulting Andrea Constand, Cosby claimed their relationship was consensual. The first trial resulted in a hung jury. Then came the Weinstein case and the sequence of events it triggered. By the time Cosby went to the courtroom again, the atmosphere was very different and the jury announced its guilty verdict after fewer than two days of deliberation.

These types of crossroads had been approached many times before. In the 1970s, second wave feminism led protests and demands for gender equality in pay, representation and rights. This time appeared to be different and, while sceptics suspected the most profound changes would be felt in the more visible entertainment industry, #MeToo was, to this writer at least, an installment rather than the whole asking price.

'Today "empowerment" invokes power while signifying the lack of it. It functions like an explorer staking a claim on new territory with a white flag.' Jia Tolentino, of the *New York Times*, was writing in April 2016, 18 months before the Weinstein case made news. Women now boast empowerment without delineating either what they mean or what they have power of or over, observed Tolentino, as if practically anything that women do is empowering in some sense. 'It's about pleasure, not power; it's individualistic and subjective, tailored to insecurity and desire. The new empowerment doesn't increase potential so much as it assures you that your potential is just fine.' Although she doesn't spell it out, she means potential should come with a health warning; possessing or expressing a capacity to develop into something or someone in the future is only that and shouldn't be confused with actually having developed into something or someone successful with tangible power.

Doing a certain kind of workout, such as HIIT (high intensity interval training), or wearing a particular make of jewelry or lingerie, getting a divorce, breastfeeding or voiding your Facebook account are the kind of things Tolentino has in mind: they're among a countless number of products and activities that are presumed to increase female power. This is a trivialization of what was once a perfectly serviceable word that denoted having authority or being strong and confident, especially in controlling one's own life and standing up for what is rightfully yours. There's nothing wrong with having personal competency, of course. But, according to Tolentino, it's replaced anything resembling genuine power.

'But wait!' you might say. 'What exactly is wrong with more and more women growing in self-assurance and asserting themselves as individuals?' Only that it's not power, Tolentino would argue – and I'm imputing responses here because she doesn't directly address this question. I'll impute again: the cleverest deception of the concept of female empowerment is that women feel empowered while they have nothing. Reason? The term has been hijacked, handed over to the marketing people and turned into a commodity that can be bought and sold on the market – like an exercise class or Pandora jewelry (which is far more affordable than the likes of Bvlgari, favored by Liz Taylor). Women's empowerment is 'highly marketable,' argues Tolentino; it's 'a glossy, dizzying product.'

We've probably all seen those Dove ad campaigns for 'Real Beauty' 'Self-esteem Project' or 'The Woman Warrior Project.' None of them promised to smooth out wrinkles, less still make them disappear; they made a virtue of flawed ordinariness by featuring models who resembled typical consumers, rather than sylphlike models with angular cheekbones and interminable legs. This would be the type of female empowerment Tolentino has in mind; it can actually be disempowering because it offers 'a series of objects and experiences you can purchase while the conditions determining who can access and accumulate power stay the same.'

The view finds support from many quarters, including Lagos, Nigeria, where media studies scholar Simidele Dosekun based her research. Women, according to many popular and academic accounts, 'are "now empowered," and celebrating and encouraging their consequent "freedom" to return to normatively feminine pursuits and to disavow feminism as no longer needed or desirable.' In her article 'For

Western Girls Only?' Dosekun argues that the postfeminism hailed by many and accepted as proof of empowerment is "a thoroughly mediated, commodified, and consumerist discourse," which is readily transnationalized via the media, commodity, and consumer connectivities that today crisscross more borders more densely and more rapidly than ever before. In other words, like Tolentino, Dosekun sees female empowerment in its monetized form – an overabundance of products all purporting to be in some way part of the postfeminist sensibility.

On this view, women who have become successful as parts of this process would include the likes of Sheryl Sandberg, who rose to prominence as Chief Operating Officer of Facebook, an organization that woke up to female empowerment suspiciously late for Tolentino: 'A company's sudden emphasis on empowerment is often a sign of something to atone for.' In its 2016 form, female empowerment is personified by million-dollar flunkies, all displaying feminist credentials and all living, breathing brands of some order, the more global, the more powerful. There's surely irony in well-paid women with minimal political involvement taking off their clothes and exhibiting themselves for money in the name of womanhood.

'[Kim] Kardashian is the apotheosis of a particular brand of largely contentless feminism, a celebratory form divorced from material politics, which makes it palatable – maybe irresistible – to the business world.' For Tolentino, Kardashian offers nothing of significance. Perhaps she misses the pleasure that she and the other Kardashians, and, for that matter, Emily Ratajkowski, and perhaps every female celebrity with a twitter following, offer an engaged audience, rapt with tales of love, sex and fatal illnesses.

Both Tolentino and Dosekun were writing before the Weinstein scandal. So what? Has the fallout, massive as it

was, made much – or any – difference to the status of
women? Women now come forward. In November 2017,
weeks after the initial reports about Weinstein, and in the
midst of a torrent of accusations of sexual abuse from
women, Victoria's Secret staged 'the world's biggest fashion
event' in Shanghai. It aired on TV in the USA and over a billion viewers from 192 countries watched women wearing
thigh-high lace-up stiletto boots, gauzelike underwear and
one diamond-encrusted bra, valued at $2 million.

'Victoria's Secret has long framed its show as being about
female empowerment: women owning their sexuality,' wrote
Vanessa Friedman in her *New York Times* review. It's a familiar narrative and, as we've seen earlier in the chapter, the
same basic rationale used by Madonna and all that have followed in her wake. The Weinstein scandal didn't affect the
event, though it might have opened a portal from one zeitgeist
to another (the last time I'll use that word in this chapter). The
timing of the event meant that questions about its propriety,
purpose and consequences were bound to be asked.

Friedman was obviously aware of the postfeminist defense.
But, even accepting that the women involved are self-aware
and enter into the experience 'with eyes wide open and alac-
rity in their hearts' and that, according to Victoria's Secret,
two out of three people watching its show are women, 'those
don't control external perception, or even ensure that anyone
will get their message.' It's a similar point to the one I made
earlier about controlling production, but not reception.
Ratajkowski acknowledged to Friedman: 'This is something
I've battled with personally and publicly' and, in an admission that elaborated on a point she made to Wolf, added:
'I've had men comment on sexy images of me online and say,
"This is empowering to you?" Ha! I just masturbated to it so
hope you feel good about yourself.'

Does this make her complicit in the continuance of an environment in which women are objectified, dehumanized or in some other way degraded to the point where their value is reduced to their sex? Or does it make her an independent free spirit, not just intelligent enough to make her own decisions and make seriously good money, but reflective enough to understand that she is being sexualized? It's the difference between being played and playing others who think they are playing you.

CHAPTER 3

MINDLESS SEX

Whitney Houston wanted to break free of the innuendo about her and Robyn Crawford, her supposed onetime lesbian lover. Daughter of gospel singer Cissy Houston and the cousin of Dionne Warwick, Whitney was discovered by record boss Clive Davis, singing in a New York club. Groomed and packaged as a mainstream singer, whose voice drew comparisons with those of Barbra Streisand and Judy Garland, Houston studiously avoided genres associated with black artists. The aim was to make her a major showbusiness entertainer, not a black entertainer.

In 1992 when aged 29, she married 23-year-old Bobby Brown, a man raised in Orchard Park, a notorious district of Boston, and who, as part of the R&B band New Edition, became known for his explosive temper, his womanizing and his penchant for recreational drugs. At first glance, it seemed a misalliance; Houston, with her sheltered church background and seeming shyness, seemed a poor match for the hellraising singer. A year after the wedding, Houston had a daughter Bobbi Kristina. Houston had met Brown in 1989 at the Soul Train Music Awards, an annual event that honors African American artists. Not yet at the peak of her success,

Houston had made seven consecutive number one records in the USA, surpassing the record set by the Beatles and the Bee Gees. So she had already made her mark. Yet at the Soul Train ceremony, the crowd booed her, ostensibly for being 'too white.'

The Bodyguard, the 1992 movie in which she played opposite Kevin Costner, turned Houston into a global superstar. The soundtrack featured her version of *I Will Always Love You*, which sold an estimated 20 million copies. And yet the Chinese whispers about her sexuality and her romance with her best friend, executive assistant and creative director Crawford continued and tormented her – and perhaps her management. Whether or not her marriage to Brown was designed to smother the rumors and perhaps ameliorate her sometimes-strained relationship with black audiences, no one can know for sure. But there's evidence that Brown became exasperated by his wife's companionship with Crawford. It's arguable his jealousy was a factor in Crawford's leaving Houston's entourage completely in 2000. Houston offered an alternative explanation: 'Something happens to a man when a woman has that much fame,' she surmised on *Oprah*. 'I tried to play it down all the time. I used to say, "I'm Mrs. Brown, don't call me Houston".'

But there were signs of conflict that, on occasion, became physical. In 2003, police responded to a domestic violence emergency call and found Houston with a bruised cheek and a cut lip. Brown subsequently turned himself in and was charged with misdemeanor battery for hitting his wife and reportedly threatening to 'beat her ass.' Their inner conflict contrasted with the image they portrayed to the media. Houston attended her husband's court hearing, left with him, arm-in-arm, and drove away singing along to the Aretha Franklin song *(You Make Me Feel Like) A Natural Woman*.

There's also evidence that Houston's health deteriorated noticeably during her marriage. In 2000, it was reported that Hawaiian airport authorities had found nearly half an ounce of marijuana in her luggage, but she and Brown boarded a plane and took off before Houston could be arrested; the charges were later dropped. Around this time, her drug use began to reveal itself in her somewhat ravaged appearance. She owned up to favoring marijuana and crack, presumably safe in the knowledge that such drugs were in such widespread use that the revelation wouldn't hurt her career; she also claimed, in an interview with Oprah, that her husband's choices were alcohol and marijuana laced with cocaine. In 2006, the *National Enquirer* published a photo of Houston's bathroom, the surfaces scattered with a crackpipe and encrusted spoons. Her marriage to Brown ended the following year. Five years later, police were called to Houston's suite in the Beverly Hilton in Los Angeles to find her face down in the bath, dead.

Historically, the entertainment industry is known for 'lavender marriages,' which were often loveless affairs in which one or both partners were homosexual or bisexual. A lavender marriage was a way of presenting an image of a respectable heterosexual partnership. The arrangement was a serviceable defence against potentially destructive gossip. Rumours abounded that Houston's tumultuous 15-year marriage with Brown was one such arrangement. Some say Brown encouraged her deleterious drug habit, while others suggest she needed little encouragement. She appeared in public on occasion bearing the marks of what appeared to be conflicts with Brown, suggesting that this was not a marriage made in heaven. But, how damaging would it have been to Houston's career had those whispers persisted unabated?

There is an interview in the July 1995 issue of *The Advocate* featuring the Italian designer Gianni Versace, head of one of the world's most celebrated and prestigious fashion houses. His clothes and jewelry were worn by A-listers and his stage designs featured by the likes of Milan's La Scala Theatre Ballet and the Béjart Ballet, of Lausanne. There were also signature lines in fragrances and licensing agreements, which, combined with other enterprises, yielded sales of over $650 million in 1994. The name Versace was synonymous with flamboyance, luxury, grandiloquence and shameless decadence and its Medusa's head crest was recognizable practically everywhere. In the interview, Versace disclosed that he was gay and had a longstanding friendship with Antonio D'Amico, whom he described as 'my companion.' It was effectively a 'coming-out,' a gesture that appears less courageous today than it was in the mid-1990s.

There's no reliable way of knowing the thought processes that lay behind Versace's decision, though there is a scene in the 2018 television miniseries *American Crime Story: The Assassination of Gianni Versace*, in which the designer announces his intentions prior to the interview to his sister, confidante and business partner Donatella (the drama was based on Maureen Orth's book *Vulgar Favors*). It is a plausible, if conjectural, account that is imagined to have taken place two years before Versace's murder in 1997. While Donatella is comfortable with her brother's sexuality, she is strongly opposed to his divulgence on purely practical grounds. 'We're opening stores where it is illegal,' she reminds him, adding doubts about whether rock stars, actors and other celebrities with whom Versace had contracts would think twice about their deals were his homosexuality to become a matter of record. 'You have forgotten how ugly the world can be.'

But Versace himself doesn't appear to be willing to suffer hypocrites. So Donatella recounts how fellow designer Perry Ellis, in the 1980s, when stricken with Aids, had to be helped to his feet by an assistant when he tried to stride down the catwalk at the conclusion of one of his shows. 'After that, people stopped buying his clothes,' she points out. '*Some* people,' Versace himself snaps back. 'A lot of people,' Donatella responds. Ellis died in 1986, and, while Donatella's warning about sales may have been legitimate for a while, the Perry Ellis label is still going strong today. So neither Ellis' death nor Versace's declaration nine years later adversely affected the overall success of their enterprises even in a cultural climate that didn't encourage diversity. But that was changing.

If any incident captures the shift in collective attitudes towards homosexuality, it was George Michael's arrest after a police sweep in Beverly Hills. An undercover officer arrested Michael whom he observed engaging in a 'lewd act' in a public washroom. This was 1998 and the media immediately pronounced the end of Michael's showbusiness career. At 34, the former Wham! singer had enjoyed a garlanded solo career; his first solo album, *Faith*, had sold more than 10 million copies. Michael had publicly lamented the death of his close friend Anselmo Feleppa from an Aids-related illness, and, though he'd never talked openly about his sexuality, several of his songs alluded to this. *Freedom, Jesus to a Child, Fastlove* and *Spinning the Wheel* were among his compositions that dealt with gay themes.

Michael revealed to the world that he was gay in the first interview following his arrest. It was on CNN. 'I feel stupid and reckless and weak for letting my sexuality be exposed that way,' he said, no doubt mindful that many British media outlets were exploiting the comic potential of the episode, none more so than the *Sun* newspaper, which featured the frontpage headline: ZIP ME UP BEFORE YOU GO-GO – a parody of the Wham! track *Wake Me Up Before You Go-Go*.

And then something surprising happened: instead of the expected penitence, with apologies for the deception and heartfelt regrets, Michael went on the attack by releasing, as his first single after the arrest, an acidly satirical *Outside*, the video for which featured Michael dressed in an LAPD officer's uniform, carrying a phallus-like baton and dancing in a public bathroom that resembled a disco. The tune sampled radio reports of his arrest. It was a self-deprecating affair, with the song's lyrics playfully suggesting he'd grown bored with indoor sex and, as the title indicates, sought excitement outside: 'I'm done with the sofa ... let's go outside.' The video, ended with the two police officers in passionate embrace, as seen through the lens of surveillance camera. The video put viewers straight into Michael's head.

It was the most original response to a gay outing in history and probably couldn't have even happened even five or six years before; that was when Houston was presenting herself as joyously married, of course; the drugs and allegations of domestic abuse became public later. But in 1998, Michael's defiantly clever riposte made him a media darling. The laughing at his expense was replaced by laughing at the ludicrousness of trying to monitor, regulate and control people's sexual proclivities in the name of decency. Michael might just as well have pushed a custard pie in the face of homophobes. Questions that might have been posed a few years before weren't even entertained, let alone asked.

Were his heterosexual female fans going to desert him? Was his record company going to abandon him? Would concertgoers snub him? Would record buyers stop buying his albums? These weren't serious enquiries. Michael's career powered on, the self-exposure a minor, farcical interlude in a career of Homeric proportions. Michael went on to sell more than 100 million records worldwide during his 35 years as a professional singer. He was found dead in bed in his

Oxfordshire home on Christmas Day 2016, aged 53. The coroner recorded natural causes.

What can we learn from three human beings, each of whom grasped for acceptance in an ugly world? Today, we might wonder why someone's sexual preferences could have any impact on their career trajectory. Were we once such a moralistic, self-righteous, narrow-minded bunch that we couldn't accept that humankind is a mixed bag of wholegrain rather than a sack full of refined, white flour? Well, yes, actually; though probably not at the time of Houston's marriage. But, for several decades before, 'the pathologization of gender expansiveness led to utter privation for individuals constructing their identity outside of the binary of heteronormativity.'

The passage is from a 2016 article by the impressively named Steven Funk and Jaydi Funk in the journal *Sexuality & Culture*. There are a few words that need clarifying before moving on, and, as some of them, will recur, it's as well to define them here. Pathologization is the state of being regarded and treated as psychologically abnormal. Gender expansiveness is a way of describing a wide variety of exceptions to the traditional binary (involving just two sexes) of men and women. So transgender, bisexual, asexual and other groups who fall outside the binary are part of the expanse. And heteronormativity denotes a worldview promoting heterosexuality as the normal and preferred sexual orientation.

The Funks argue that restrictions on people whose sexual predilections lay outside the traditional binary meant they suffered adversity if their tastes were known and private, anguish if they concealed them. The USA had begun repealing its sodomy laws in 1971 and, in Great Britain, homosexual acts were decriminalized by the Sexual Offences Act of 1967. But any progress made in the 1960s and 1970s was undone in the 1980s when the 'gay plague,' as Aids was often called, was defined by some as retribution rather than disease. It was not a sickness likely to engender compassion from those who regarded it as a payback for promiscuous homosexuality. Aids was regarded as much a moral pestilence as a treatable medical condition.

Some gay men and women made a practical accommodation to both the cultural and legal prohibitions on homosexuality, while others endured the torment of the damned. Elton John had established his presence with a number of successful singles, seven number one albums in the US and several concert tours by 1975. Then his career appeared to crater. Many attributed this to a 1976 cover interview he gave *Rolling Stone*, in which he talked about his being bisexual to writer Cliff Jahr: 'There's nothing wrong with going to bed with somebody of your own sex. I think everybody's bisexual to a certain degree. I don't think it's just me. It's not a bad thing to be.'

In 1984, with panic over Aids escalating, he married Renate Blauel, a female sound engineer. The wedding on Valentine's Day in Sydney, Australia, suggested he had swung towards the hetero end of the pendulum arc. The marriage would last four years after which John admitted, 'I was living a lie.' It proved an expedient falsehood. In the year before the divorce, John had released *Blue Eyes, I'm Still Standing* and *I Guess That's Why They Call it the Blues*, three of his most memorable and commercially successful tracks.

Today, it's difficult to think of Elton John in a straight marriage or even trying to convince anyone he was anything other than gay. He was conspicuously accompanied by his future husband David Furnish at the funeral of Diana, Princess of Wales, in 1997. Earlier in 1992, he'd established the Elton John AIDS Foundation. But, like the majority of gay men in showbusiness, he must have been uncertain about the consequences of making known his sexuality. Most were engaged in a performance.

Liberace (1919–1987), the singer-pianist known for his effeteness and flamboyance of manner and dress, went to his grave an ostensibly straight man and took legal action against those who even intimated otherwise.

Hollywood's epitome of heterosexual manhood Rock Hudson (1925–1985), whose onscreen pursuit of Doris Day helped create the genre we now call romcom, married his agent's secretary Phyllis Gates in one of those lavender arrangements I mentioned earlier. Both performers died from Aids-related illnesses. Clifton Webb (1889–1966) was unexceptional in many respects; mostly a support actor rather than headliner, he was probably best known for his role in the 1944 film noir *Laura*. But, in another respect, he was exceedingly exceptional: an inveterate bachelor, whose sexual tastes were wellknown in the film industry, but rarely beyond. The industry's reluctance to acknowledge anything but the straightest of straight sexual orientations led to a kind of purdah. Webb, despite a career spent on the cast credits rather than the opening titles did star in one movie, that being the 1953 version of *Titanic*, directed by Jean Negulesco. This engendered a popular insider gag: 'Did you hear? Clifton Webb went down on the *Titanic*.'

Few actors other than Webb were brave enough to allow their sexual proclivities to remain ambiguous. Stephen Vider, in 2012, argued that some actors, such as Randolph Scott and Cary Grant, in their unusually close friendship, 'expanded the boundaries of appropriate and 'normal' male behavior.' But this didn't undermine their heterosexual credentials during their acting careers.

Straightness was the *sine qua non* of a successful career in showbusiness up till the late 1990s and, while no one is scattering the ashes of homophobia (or, for that matter, any other kind of sex-related phobia) yet, a willingness to embrace, respect or perhaps just tolerate individual rights and freedoms, a broadening of knowledge and experience of others from different backgrounds and with different faiths as well as sensibilities and a concern with the wellbeing and protection of others who have been historically mistreated, oppressed or persecuted has put irrational fears, aversions and bigotries under pressure. As I say, no one is scattering the ashes yet awhile. But the liberalization is self-evident in practically every sphere of society. There are openly gay people, male and female, in politics, entertainment, commerce, public services and most sports; they go about their business mostly without interference.

Biology may not be destiny, but history appears to be; you'd swear events that have been happening since the 1960s were necessary and uncontrollable. How could a society that purported to be civilized, or at least in the process of civilizing, deny, suppress and punish groups who didn't occupy a preordained position on the sexual landscape? *If you're a woman, stand over there. Man? Drop your pants and let me see. OK, stand over there!* If this was civilization, it was one that refused civil rights of social freedom to an unknown number of citizens. The change that led to the cultural environment we recognize today has its origins in the 1960s, but picked up pace in the early 1990s.

The Stonewall riots, of 1969, revealed a hitherto undisclosed militancy among gay men and women when they demonstrated in the Manhattan neighborhood, Greenwich Village. The unrest started spontaneously after a routine police raid on The Stonewall Inn, a bar frequented by patrons of many sexual orientations. After this, several gay organizations were launched, their aim being to give gays the voice of believable people with legitimate complaints, as opposed to queers (a term that was later appropriated, redeemed and fused with positive connotations).

How would a good Christian interpret the advocacy for cultural and legal changes that have affected our experience of sexuality? Writing for the Roman Catholic journal *New Oxford Review* in 2016, Tom Bethell summarized a typical advocates' recommendations:

> *The enshrinement of same-sex marriage into law; the urgent need to keep abortion legal (it's a "women's issue," we are told); the (absurd) claim that there are no real differences between the sexes (claimed differences are mere "cultural constructs"); the demonizing of all criticism of homosexuality (replacing a taboo against defending it); and the pretence that we are free to change our gender anytime we wish.*

This makes a decent digest, in my view, though the bracketed annotations make Bethell's stance vividly apparent and no one actually pretends that anyone is 'free' to change their gender at a time of their own choosing; though, in some circumstances, children and adults have adjusted their appearance in a way that suits their self-identity and asked to be treated as members of a different gender to the one to which they were assigned at birth. In spite of this, Bethell's précis is serviceable, and his parenthetical comments a reliable guide to how many sections of society reacted to the changes or the calls for further change after 1969.

With Ronald Reagan and Margaret Thatcher both vanquished, the Iron Curtain torn asunder and South African apartheid dismantled by 1991, the dubious political and cultural endowments of the 1980s were left behind. Between Whitney Houston's marriage (1992) and George Michael's arrest (1998), Bill Clinton, Tony Blair and Nelson Mandela rose to power, the distinct, if delicate optimism of Generation

X emerged and an effective treatment for HIV and Aids was discovered and approved. Fifteen years of research had failed to find a cure, but in 1996, a combination of three or more drugs that stop the HIV virus from replicating, known as antiretroviral therapy, was the breakthrough that led to normal life expectancy for those living with the condition.

Sex as a cultural construct; this was the suggestion – or was it a recommendation? – to which Bethell objected. Yet it was to inspire a sirocco of cultural changes that blew through the 1990s into the twenty-first century. With hindsight the proposition that sex, like race, illness, happiness and other features of humanity, is a product of human agreement is still controversial. We negotiate a way of defining something and decide how we should address or engage with it; then, over time, we forget our own authorship and think of them as things: objective things. I'm mindful of the perils of being too didactic, but a brief detour into medical history should clarify the argument.

In what respects are men and women different? This strikes us as perfectly obvious. But the fact that it *does seem* obvious illustrates how dramatically our understanding of human differences can change. In the eighteenth and nineteenth centuries, curiosity in the medical world centered on the physical dissimilarities between women and men, the former being quite fragile by comparison with their robust counterparts. Medical historian Thomas Lacqueur's inspection of medical texts revealed what seems today a barely believable finding: that the concept of a sharp division between male and female became an accepted fact about 350 years ago and, for 2,000 years before that, bodies were not visualized in terms of differences at all. Take a moment to think about this: the binary division of the world into men and women based on sex is a relatively new convention and, historically, there were just people, some of whom were capable of bearing children and others who couldn't.

Nowadays, people laugh if you suggest sexuality is more of a kaleidoscope than a salt and pepper set. They will probably point to the obvious physical difference. But it's how we make sense of those differences that dictates our understanding. For example, in some periods, a woman's clitoris was thought to be an underdeveloped version of the equivalent structure in men – the penis. For most of human history, similarities rather than differences between women and men were more interesting 'with the female body simply an inverted version of the male,' as Jeffrey Weeks put it in his 2003 book *Sexuality*.

It barely needs stating, but this vision supplemented and strengthened an androcentric worldview – focused on men, in other words. 'Man is the measure of all and things and woman does not exist as an ontologically distinct category,' wrote Laqueur in his book *Making Sex: Body and Gender from the Greeks to Freud*. Sex wasn't just a property of reproductive organs: it affected every part of the body and, according to some, the mind. This doesn't mean there was institutionalized concealment orchestrated by a mendaciously patriarchal medical profession (as some might argue). But it does suggest that science, like everything else, is a cultural pursuit and, as such, reflects and affects the world that surrounds it.

Londa Schiebinger's medical history *The Mind Has No Sex: Women in the Origins of Modern Science* traces how anatomists in the nineteenth century were preoccupied not only by what made women different, but by the sources of their apparent inferiority. The female skull was supposed to 'prove' that women were naturally the subordinates of men in an intellectual sense. The concept of sexual difference seeped into every aspect of discourse, so that, by the end of the nineteenth century, we'd arrived at the basic understanding that proved serviceable for the whole of the following century. Female and male bodies were opposites, each having different organs, skeletons, functions and feelings.

Medical science transformed our understanding: the reason for the difference between women and men didn't reveal itself slowly; it arrived in an instant when a discovery in 1902 offered a way figuring out why bodies developed differently. Hormones were the chemical substances secreted in glands that determined and regulated bodily behavior – and, according to some, mood. In her book *Beyond the Natural Body: An Archeology of Sex Hormones*, Nelly Oudshoorn shows that new knowledge didn't just make the human body more comprehensible and transparent: it altered its nature – nature being the sense we impose on our physical environment to help us make sense of it.

The binary, as we know it today, took shape over the next thirty years after the crucial discovery. As these decades passed, endocrinology (the branch of medicine focused on hormones) established a conception of sexual difference based on hormones and this was accepted as scientific orthodoxy. Knowledge doesn't just zip into our minds out of nowhere: it's discovered and interpreted, then shaped in a way that helps us make otherwise puzzling things intelligible. The hormonal conception of sexual difference was adopted universally and defined the contours of practically every debate on women in the twentieth century and beyond. Science doesn't lie: women were different to men in a clear-cut and permanent way. This was how we interpreted the reality that confronted us. We could always reinterpret it. We did.

'I grew up in a country that allowed me to do what I wanted to do,' Bruce Jenner told the *New York Times*' Dave

Anderson in 1976 (July 31). He'd just become the ninth American to win the Olympic decathlon title. In the process, he'd broken the world record. In the interludes between the 10 events, Jenner had worn a gray tee-shirt emblazoned with an instruction: 'FEET, don't fail me now.' As Anderson responded: 'They didn't. Neither did his arms and his legs and his torso and his heart.' Peggy Shinn later reflected: 'With an infectious smile, Atlas-like physique, shaggy hair, charming personality and ability to slay his Soviet foe in the midst of the Cold War, Jenner became a real-life superhero.'

In the early interview with Anderson, Jenner said: 'I've built up a lot of credibility as an athlete and I don't want to do anything to tarnish that,' meaning that he didn't intend to re-map his career as a serial endorser and all-round celebrity, as other successful athletes were starting to do in the 1970s (and which they still do, of course). But he couldn't escape the publicity. Jenner became, as the *Washington Post*'s Emily Yahr described him in 2015, 'the buff heartthrob of America's disco era' and his image began to appear in ads for all manner of product, including Wheaties breakfast cereal.

In a sense he was a symbol of American masculinity. He divorced his wife, with whom he had two children, in 1981 and married the actor, beauty queen and former Elvis consort Linda Thompson the same year; they also had two children. Their marriage lasted till 1986. By this time, Jenner had succumbed to the very lifestyle he said he wanted to avoid and was a regular on TV and film dramas. Jenner married for a third time in 1991. His wife was Kris Kardashian, formerly married to Robert Kardashian, a lawyer, who was later to represent OJ Simpson at his epochal trial; they had four children.

A month after her divorce from Robert Kardashian, Kris married Jenner, by now long retired from sports and earning well from celebrity-oriented assignments. They had two girls,

Kendall, born in 1995, and Kylie, born 1997. The Jenners announced their separation after 22 years of marriage in 2013 and Kris filed for divorce the next year, citing irreconcilable differences. But not before both had become stars of *Keeping Up With the Kardashians*, the illustrious reality show that launched on the E! channel in 2007.

When Jenner won his Olympic gold medal, there was no such thing as gender dysphoria; and, if there were, no one would have taken it seriously. It describes the condition of feeling one's identity, psychologically and emotionally as male or female, as not the same as one's biological sex. A gender dysphoric person is often said to be living in the wrong body and, while for long their response would be simply to endure and adapt, transformative surgery has been available since the 1920s. Danish painter Lili Elbe (born Einar Wegener), whose life story was fictionalized in the film *The Danish Girl*, had five surgeries performed as part of her male-to-female transition but died from infection-related complications of her final surgery in 1931. The first American to undergo a sex change operation was Christine Jorgensen (also the subject of a film), who made headlines in the *New York Times* in 1952: 'BRONX "BOY" IS NOW A GIRL' (December 2). The former army clerk went to Denmark for the treatment, which is now known as sex reassignment surgery, or SRS.

Three years before the Stonewall riots, a cafeteria in San Francisco's red light district was the scene of a less-publicized upheaval; police raided Gene Compton's Cafeteria, which was a haunt of predominantly African American drag queens – male sex workers dressed ostentatiously in women's clothes – and transgender women. Actually, the word transgender wasn't used in the 1960s; they would have been called transvestites if they just dressed as women, and transsexuals if they'd had reassignment treatment. 'Female impersonation' was an arrestable offense (and was, in many parts of the US, until the twenty-first century).

Richard Raskind was not a major player in sports; a so-so tennis player, he captained Yale University's tennis team in the late 1950s. In the 1960s, he traveled in Europe and assumed the identity of a woman, but without undertaking reassignment surgery. In 1975, when back in the US, he opted for surgery and resumed life as Renée Clark. At 40, Clark moved to California and started competing in tennis tournaments; her 6 feet 2 inch (1.88 meters) frame and booming ground shots gave her an advantage over all but the best women. After she won the La Jolla Tennis Tournament in July 1976, a journalist reported that she had previously competed as a man.

Predictably, there was resistance to Clark, or Richards, as she later called herself. But she gained entry to the 1977 US Open, while in her forties. Richards eventually won her case against the US Tennis Association, which had opposed her right to play professional tennis as a woman. She later acknowledged: 'I became a public figure, a reluctant pioneer, for all of the disenfranchised groups in the world, no matter whether they were transgender, gay or lesbian.'

Much of the excitement about celebrity culture is that no one knows what's next – but, whatever or whoever it is, you can be sure there will be cameras around. In January 2014, Jenner, his neck bandaged after a tracheal shave, was caught on camera and the resulting picture whirled around the world courtesy of social media. He'd already been taking hormones, had undergone two rhinoplasties and been growing his head hair while depilating his body hair. (Later he would opt for breast augmentation, but not for genital surgery; there's a misperception that genital removal is required to be a transgender woman. A tracheal shave is a common surgical procedure favored by men wishing to look more like women;

it involves reducing the thyroid cartilage of the larynx so that the Adam's apple is not so prominent.)

After splitting with Kris, Jenner remained in the public glare and the discernible changes in his physical appearance fed rumors. In the week prior to his 65th birthday in October 2014, Kris Jenner appeared on television and dismissed as 'silly' any suggestions that her soon-to-be ex-husband was becoming a woman. Bruce had been romantically linked to Kris' former assistant and longtime friend Ronda Kamihira. The mystery deepened.

People might have been appalled or perhaps repulsed by the Richards case that rumbled through the 1970s, but responses to gender switching were more relaxed in 2014. By then Laverne Cox had become the first African American trans-gender woman to produce and star in her own TV show TRANSform Me, and later starred in *Orange is the New Black* (2013), appearing on the cover of *Time* in 2014; Kye Allums had become the first openly trans man to play NCAA basket-ball (for George Washington University, 2011) and Miss Universe reversed an earlier ruling and allowed Canadian con-testant Jenna Talackova into the competition in 2012. Other areas of society weren't allowed to sit still, while attitudes towards gay men and women were recast; perspectives on groups with other sexual orientations or convictions were also changing.

ABC Television, in April 2015, featured a two-hour edi-tion of its *20/20* program in which Diane Sawyer interviewed Bruce Jenner and in which he (the program used the mascu-line pronoun) occasionally referred to himself in the third person. He called himself heterosexual and was attracted to women, but identified as a woman. During the interview, he revealed that, this wasn't a recent epiphany; for five years in the 1980s, he had taken estrogen and received electrolysis to remove hair. When he ceased, he said, it was because he suspected his children would be affected by a transition. Three months later, he was interviewed by Buzz Bissinger in *Vanity Fair* (July 2015). 'He needed credibility to squelch the rumors, and he told me marrying Kris Kardashian, in 1991, helped give him that along with compatibility and love,' wrote Bissinger, still using the male pronoun despite the caption across the cover picture of Jenner, 'Call Me Caitlyn.'

'We're gonna change the world,' Jenner had told Sawyer expressively, as if the emergence from the chrysalis of self-conscious womanhood was the start of a movement rather than an individual's quest for an alignment of body and mind. Jenner's appearances on *20/20*, dressed in men's clothes, and on *Vanity Fair* in an ivory-colored satin corset (styled by Jessica Diehl, the magazine's fashion and style director), weren't received uniformly. Hunter Felt, of the *Guardian*, seemed to speak for the majority when venturing Jenner 'showed true courage' and deserved 'the world's praise.'

Germaine Greer, a stalwart feminist presence since the 1970s, was less laudatory about the newly-emerging trans-gender movement: 'Just because you lop off your dick and then wear a dress doesn't make you a fucking woman.' Greer's public lectures and appearances were picketed and some canceled. In the same statement Greer declared: 'I do understand that some people are born intersex and they deserve support in coming to terms with their gender but it's not the same thing.' Intersex is the condition of having both male and female sex organs and other sexual characteristics, such as hormones and an intersex person was defined in 2015 by the UN Commissioner for Human Rights as anyone born with 'sex characteristics ... that do not fit typical binary notions of male or female bodies.'

Then a septuagenarian and unafraid to make new enemies, Greer suggested in an interview on the BBC's *Newsnight* program, the acclaim garnered by Jenner was not only undeserved but misogynistic, her logic presumably being: people who had transitioned male-to-female were being elevated to a status above that of those born as biologically female. Daniel Harris also offered a grimly mocking appraisal, not just of Jenner but of all transgender persons, which he abbreviated to TG: 'Sex reassignment is the logical outcome of an excess of heterosexuality, of a love for women so intense that the straight TG tries to transform himself into the object of his desire.'

His article 'The Sacred Androgen,' while unrelentingly sarcastic in tone, contrives to make several points about the culture that applauded Jenner's decision, particularly the exaggeration of the power of our freewill: 'Biological facts are mere opportunities to strengthen this hypertrophied will, hurdles to overcome on one's journey to "self-actualization".' All of us are now products of what Harris called 'a self-help culture, in which the will is all-powerful, in which one can be anything one chooses simply by dint of effort, leaping over such obstacles as fate, destiny, necessity, and chance to create "an entirely new you".'

Jenner's public acknowledgment of her transition was straight from the Theater of Kardashian, that is drama departing from conventional dramatic form to portray a feature of human life, but in a way that shakes, confounds and leaves audiences open-mouthed. When they recover composure, the audience can reexamine their own, possibly orthodox assumptions. Like so many other Kardashian exploits, Jenner's provided a framing device for the countless other dramas, including the ones we have covered in these pages.

Since the mid-1990s, there has been what Molly Fischer, of *New York* magazine describes as 'a growing acceptance, especially among a broad swath of young people, of easy gender fluidity and ambiguity.' One way to test this is by looking at Facebook: in 2014, it changed its gender options from the basic two to a choice of 50. These included neutrois, gender-queer and cis. (In case you're not *au fait*: the first – pronounced *new-twhah* – means having no fixed gender identity at all; the second refers to having a combination of gender characteristics; the third denotes having a personal and gender identity that corresponds with the birth sex). In 2015, Facebook decided the proliferation of gender labels had become unmanageable, so abandoned the preset menu completely. Instead it let users pick up to 10 terms of their own choosing, or creation.

'We find ourselves poised someplace between gender mattering tremendously and mattering not very much at all,' reflects Fischer. Or, if we're going to be consistent with the fluidity everywhere else, perhaps it both matters and doesn't matter. Excuse the apparent sophistry. But every day you check the news you'll find a story of some kind that has practical consequences for the way we understand sex and gender. What's more it doesn't surprise us to learn that there are gender neutral bathrooms, or that the president of a rugby organization is a woman, who used to be a man, or that we are even using terms like heteronormativity, let alone criticizing anything or anybody seen to be upholding it. Fischer calls it 'the impulse to examine assumptions' and I think this is the nearest we can get to capturing the changes witnessed since the 1990s. The kind of lavender marriages of the twentieth century, the coming-out interviews and the tabloid-ready exposés are things of the past. Yet, on the evidence we regularly receive from many sources, we can't say the same thing about the phobias and the acts of venom directed at those outside the two conventional areas of the sexual kaleidoscope. Homophobia, transphobia and intersexphobia (or interphobia, as it's sometimes called) persist, even if their life force has been draining for the past few decades – and will probably continue to drain.

This sounds optimistic. But consider: everyone is normal now. Equally, every person is dysfunctional in some way or other. This is just a feature of what Zygmunt Bauman (1925–2017) called *Liquid Life*: it's uncertain, precarious and has the consistency of, well, liquid. In other words, its molecular substance flows rather than fits into slots, categories or fractions. This sounds like another unbearable, post-ironic contribution to our non-understanding of society. Imagine though: a 'society in which the conditions under which its members act change faster than it takes the ways of acting to consolidate into habits and routines.'

For some, the lack of certainty detected by Bauman must sound like a waking nightmare. Surely we all have an identity, a fixed and permanent sense of who we are and what we like, whom we love, where our interests lie and why we believe the things we do. Maybe once, Bauman would reply. Today a self-conception that remains coherent and manageable over time – and, for that matter, space – is just something psychologists assume exists.

I recall, in the early 1980s, reading a book by the sociologist Kenneth Plummer with the fascinating title *The Making of the Modern Homosexual*. 'Making' suggested there was process of development or manufacture in producing something. That was Plummer's intention: to reveal how there is nothing natural or innate about 'the homosexual'; the term is an invention and a relatively recent one at that. Plummer spared readers the usual taxonomies and categories, instead deepening our understanding of how humanity rarely fits into parcels, but instead undergoes experiences. Instead of writing about sexuality as if it were a thing, Plummer encouraged us to approach it as an uncertainly limned experience, an experience that changes just as we change.

Plummer wrote this before the new world of the early 1990s intensified our pursuit of true selves, as well as of commodities, fame and distinction. But Plummer gave an answer to a question he didn't even ask: what happens when we denature sex? Because that's effectively what's happened over the past several decades. Gender was always in a different shopping aisle: since its separation from a strictly grammatical term to a political one in the 1970s, gender has been considered social or cultural rather than biological and, in this sense, it was a construct denoting a range of identities that usually, but not necessarily, correspond to the established binary of male and female.

In the 1990s, the philosopher Judith Butler conceived of gender in a similar way to what linguists call performativity: this is an utterance by which a speaker performs an act, such as 'I bet,' or 'I promise.' In other words, the action of speaking the phrase does something that changes reality rather than just describe it. Gender, said Butler, wasn't something people possess; it was something they *did*, over and over again. A performance, rather like a dramatic or artistic performance, except without a script but which characterized a social or cultural role. It was an influential idea: that we continually performed our gender roles and, in the process, perpetuated the reality of gender. No one actually compelled us to do so; but society's institutional arrangements made it troublesome to deviate.

Now, it seems, those arrangements have been destabilized, though this doesn't mean the performance had stopped. You, reader, are performing gender right now. But sex is something different. It used to be regarded as natural, fixed-from-birth and, in many ways, quite separable from gender. Now this too has escaped its natural habitat and roams in a cultural landscape amok with wildlife. Plummer would predict that, we'll acquire new meanings of sex; in other words, how to act, feel and be sexual. These are not lessons with a syllabus. There are many ways of interpreting or making sense of sex and we're continually learning new ways. There are *Cosmopolitan Sexualities*, as the title of one of Plummer's later books expresses it.

Jess Cartner-Morley, of the *Guardian*, in 2015, rhapsodized: 'The first family of the reality TV generation have, with the Jenner story, become catalysts for progressive social change.' She had a point because Jenner, though barracked by some, was generally thought to have forced us to explore sex from multiple angles in much the same way as George Michael and the other figures covered in this chapter did. In another era, their experiences could have been read as cautionary tales about deeply flawed people. Instead they were more like parables that we discussed and argued over.

When people think the Kardashians have hit a new peak of triviality, they should remind themselves that their meaningless escapades sometimes turn into what Cartner-Morley calls 'something positive, progressive and meaningful.' She adds that a Kim Kardashian tweet has 'more impact on cultural mores than any number of obscure activists preaching the same thing.'

Sex is becoming – or perhaps has already become – what gender has been all along: a cultural construct. I used this term earlier and I'll use it again later without apology. I hope to show it's not just a barbarous misuse of language, but a reminder that much of what we take as natural is, on closer inspection, our own primitivist invention. When the writer and sex therapy supervisor Margaret Nichols concluded in 2016, 'the boundaries between male and female are getting fuzzier and fuzzier,' what she actually meant is that they're looking fuzzier to us because, in our minds, there were once clear, distinct boundaries and we're now adjusting our focus.

We're willing to complicate our understanding. Sex is neither binary nor inseparable from gender: it's just that we used to see it that way.

You might think binary sex categories and gender differences are heading the same way as superstitions, analogue TVs and coalmining. But the 'fuzzier and fuzzier' scenario glimpsed by Nichols may not materialize and will certainly not diffuse to other areas of society where there are groups we're not sure whether to hate or embrace. We live in a time when difference, diversity and deviance are still considered destabilizing, but being unstable isn't such a bad thing: it means we're more likely to respond to change.

Self-appointed sexuality is now commonplace. Children, who move across the binary, are often assisted by parents and schools. A mother in Kansas has told how she lets her six-year-old transgender son live as a little girl called Tracy. The school makes a reasonable adjustment to accommodate her, while Tracy has therapy at a gender pathways clinic where a psychologist helps her understand her identity. An even younger child in England was diagnosed with gender dysphoria when aged four and switched from Zachary to Zachy. The child's primary school (for children between the ages of about 5 and 11 in the UK) supported the mother's decision and allowed Zachy, a natal male, to wear a girl's school uniform and her hair in pigtails. In many areas of society, a medical diagnosis isn't necessary: gender fluidity requires little apart from a subjective evaluation. Institutional support typically follows. (Legislation on transgender status differs around the world.)

There are cases in which people feel comfortable dressing as and being treated as a female in some contexts, but not others. It sounds hectic and confusing, but if the person wishes to dispense with a coherent, uniform sexuality, then we have a world ready to accommodate them. There is a summer camp in San Francisco specifically for gender fluid children as young as four. Charlize Theron (in 2016) and Megan Fox (in 2017) allowed their sons to dress as Elsa from the film *Frozen* for parties. They were among many parents who let their sons wear costumes, and the nasty reaction from some quarters reminds us not to get too carried away.

By the way, Disney's film was regarded by some as a document of gender fluidity: not one but two princesses, neither fitting into the stereotype; love-at-first sight revealed as nonsense; a handsome prince who turns out to be a bad guy; a same-sex couple with giggling children; a denouement that features sisterhood being preferred to conventional romantic love. By dispensing with gender roles, it introduced a fluidity rarely seen, certainly not in Disney's oeuvre. (Predictably, it didn't please everyone. 'Elsa is just a variation on the archetypal power-hungry female villain whose lust for power replaces lust for a mate and who threatens the patriarchal status quo,' wrote professors Madeline Streiff and Lauren Dunes of the film's lead character, in the journal *Social Sciences*. But Lucinda Everett, of the *Guardian*, concluded that the film, after its release in 2013, 'sparked hefty debate and hearty praise from critics, academics, parents, and equal rights campaigners.')

That's Disney, not real life (though, of course, even animated characters have to be relatable). The term 'gender fluid' sounds sweet and syrupy, but it's a bit too simplified and doesn't tell us whether we should expect a gentle babbling brook or a destructive flood, or even, a maelstrom. If sex and gender are, as I've argued, liquefied, everything else is too. To understand culture as anything but an ever-changing, shape-shifting flow means to attribute false stability and easy categorization.

CHAPTER 4

APPROPRIATE BLACKNESS

Your name is Nkechi Amare. It used to be Rachel. And you're a rarity: a woman who is publicly denounced for saying you're black and proud. Up till 2015, everything in your life seemed peachy. You worked part-time at Eastern Washington University's Africana-studies program, and were president of the Spokane chapter of the National Association for the Advancement of Colored People, or NAACP to use its abbreviation.

You were, by common consent, an effective civil rights advocate, having researched African American history, culture and politics meticulously. You're also a respectable portraiture artist. But since 2015, you've suffered what seems a fate worse than death. At a time when most people expected the news cycle would be dominated by the news that Donald Trump would run for the US presidency, the hatchet job on you was the big story. So what happened?

Let's start with what we know for certain: you were born in 1977 and raised in Troy, Montana, by your parents, Ruthanne and Larry, both evangelical Christians. While studying at Belhaven University, in Mississippi, you petitioned for the first annual celebration of Martin Luther King

Jr Day and helped develop the first African American history course on campus. After graduating, you moved to Washington DC to attend Howard University, the private doctoral, research-based institution where the majority of the administration, staff, faculty and students are African American. From its foundation in 1867, Howard has been nonsectarian, but, historically, it's gained a reputation as a predominantly black university. The university doesn't require members to register their ethnic origin.

You got married in 2000 to Kevin Moore; the marriage lasted till 2005. You served as chair of the volunteer citizen Police Ombudsman Commission in Spokane; this agency provides independent citizen perspectives on the police in the area. In September 2009, you filed a report to the police stating that you'd found a noose on your front door a few days after your house was robbed. You also claimed you'd had several problems with Aryan Nation and other far-right groups because of your job and, as the police report stated, your 'biracial heritage.'

There's nothing exceptional about any of this, of course. You're clearly an actively engaged woman, who feels passionately about injustice and persecution and is prepared to fight for what you think is right. You're quoted as saying: 'I will never stop fighting for human rights.' And then it happened.

At 37, long divorced from your husband and bringing up three sons, you'd established a reputation and were a prominent and effective NAACP leader, speaking regularly in the media, particularly about the cases of racism, when Ruthanne and Larry went on a local Spokane news channel and spoke about you. 'Rachel has wanted to be somebody she's not. She's chosen not to just be herself, but to represent herself as an African American woman or a biracial person and that's simply not true,' Ruthanne submitted.

Of course, having an African American origin wasn't a prerequisite for your job. 'One's racial identity is not a qualifying criteria or disqualifying standard for NAACP leadership,' the national group pointed out. But the 'not true' part of the statement stung. You've lived most of your life as a black woman, coiffured your hair in cornrows and other styles associated with black people and invited others to treat you as an African American, without giving them occasion to ask, 'Are you really black? Or are you just *passing?*' In other words, claiming to be black when you are really white.

Your most fundamental response was that you didn't *deceive* anybody. You have never claimed to be African American. But you said and still say you are black. You maintain, 'There's a difference in those terms.' I think I know what you mean. Others don't; they equate the two and consider you a fraud. You reckon your colleagues at the NAACP are 'supportive,' but let's face it, this story has gone global and it's become embarrassing. So much so that you feel compelled to resign your position. You'll survive, of course. On your own admission, the skills you perfected in creating your identity as a black woman, equip you well.

A few months later, when the *cause célèbre* had died down somewhat, Rihanna offered her thoughts about you: 'She kind of flipped on society a little bit,' she told Julie Miller of *Vanity Fair*. 'Is it such a horrible thing that she pretended to be black? Black is a great thing, and I think she legit changed people's perspective a bit and woke people up.'

Others failed to see the benefit. The *Independent*'s Nishaat Ismail seemed to echo the thoughts of many when she labeled you, 'the disgraced former NAACP president who lied about being black.' According to Ismail: 'As well as losing her livelihood, she has been rejected and shunned by the African American community she found belonging with, as well as plenty of white friends.'

The baiting hasn't budged you. You continue to proclaim your blackness and, as if to show you're unafraid of your critics, legally changed your name to Nkechi Amare Diallo. This presumably means that your former name is no more, at least in a legal sense. But I suspect we can't just magic the old name out of existence. The debate you started about the status of blackness will persist and the question you asked, however inadvertently, about whether self-willed ethnicity is equatable with 'naturally' endowed ethnicity, will stay fresh for the foreseeable future. Any attempt to answer it will certainly involve the Rachel Dolezal case.

People who attempt self-reinvention are either praised to the skies or dragged through the mud. Daniel Harris offered an example. 'When Rachel Dolezal goes to the Palm Beach tanning salon for her weekly $30 dip, she is committing the unconscionable crime of appropriating blackness,' wrote Harris, in his 2016 essay 'The Sacred Androgen.' 'When Laverne Cox, one of the breakout performers on the television show *Orange Is the New Black*, slaps on a transdermal estrogen patch, she is lauded as a hero and role model.'

The rules governing popular responses to ethnic transmutation are different, dramatically different, to those governing responses to sex and gender transition. Harris wonders why. He reckons the excessive respect given to people who try to convert the body hormonally or surgically because of unease or dissatisfaction with their natal sex contrasts weirdly with the condemnation that typically meets people who even seem to want to change ethnicity. Michael Jackson (1958–2009) is an example of the latter, of course. Though his autopsy confirmed he suffered from vitiligo, a skin condition in which the pigment is lost from areas of the skin, causing whitish patches, the popular theory was that he was anguished by his dark skin and sought to lighten it. The plastic surgery procedures he elected to undergo added substance to this, of course.

Jackson was among many African Americans who have been scolded for even giving the impression they'd tried to hide or expunge their skin color. In 2008, L'Oréal presented images of Beyoncé that seemed to have been digitally altered to make her facial skin appear whiter in ads. *TMZ*, on August 6, 2008 described the Beyoncé images as 'bleached out,' launching an online poll to decide if the whitening was 'a slap to blacks?' Among the responses was: 'Shame on Beyoncé.'

Kerry Washington's skin was lightened for the April 4, 2015 cover of *Adweek*, though the magazine's editorial director owned up to only 'minimal adjustments, solely for the cover's design needs,' according to Martha Ross, of the *San Jose Mercury* (April 6, 2016).

Azealia Banks probably knew she would kick up a social media storm when she went on Instagram and Facebook Live video to announce she used skin-lightening agents as a way of assimilating (her word), in 2016. The singer/songwriter from Harlem defended the practice: 'What's the difference between getting a nose job and changing your skin color?' The pushback didn't deter her. Later, she defended Kim Kardashian, when she was criticized for braiding her hair in a style popularly associated with African Americans: 'Why are black folk as mad [at] Kim Kardashian's braids … It's just hair.'

And yet the rapturous reception for Caitlyn Jenner after she'd switched washrooms was very different. She'd liberated her inner woman, escaped the prison of her natal body and faced up to her true identity. There was, it seemed, something almost superhumanly valiant about Jenner's transformation. *Ebony* described Dolezal as 'like some sort of cultural fungus' (May 9, 2016).

In Western culture, sex and race were traditionally considered natural and unchangeable. In the eighteenth, nineteenth and part of the twentieth centuries, the concept of race in particular was regarded in scientific circles as one of the principal divisions of mankind (as the world's population would have been collectively known). Everyone belonged to a race, which was fixed from birth. Following the Second World War, UNESCO, the agency of the United Nations set up to promote the exchange of ideas, issued a strong statement, clarifying the evidence, historical and contemporary, scientific and cultural, on race. Its conclusion was that race was largely mythical and had no basis in reality. Humans did not slot into natural groups with immutable differences and most of the observable differences are the result of cultural factors.

The statement was released in 1950; a half-century later in 2000, Craig Venter, the pioneer of DNA sequencing, reinforced the point: 'The concept of race has no genetic or scientific basis' (he's quoted in a *National Geographic* article by Elizabeth Kolbert, 'There's No Scientific Basis for Race – It's a Made-Up Label'). Race remains a potent member of everyday vocabulary and, despite every attempt to undermine it, lives on, if only in the imagination. Race isn't about credibility or fact: it's just a term that fires us into life whenever we hear it.

We heard it many times in 2015 when Dolezal's story made news. 'Race of Rachel Dolezal, head of Spokane NAACP, comes under question' reported *CNN International* (June 15). The British *Daily Mail* called Dolezal a 'Race faker' (December 14). 'Is changing one's *race* a sign of mental health problems?' asked the online magazine *The Conversation US* (December 16). It's unlikely that Dolezal was not familiar with the redundancy of the race concept. She was pretty clear when she told Patt Morrison, of the

Los Angeles Times, in 2017 'Race is a social construct, even if we don't want it to be' (March 8).

She was quite specific about not masquerading as an African American. This is a term that's used synonymously with black, though not by all. Barack Obama, for example, called himself an African American, his father being a Kenyan. Beyoncé studiously avoided designations completely until 2016. Dolezal didn't seek a mandate for her distinction, but she could probably have found several. For instance, black as an adjective for African Americans was an insult up to the mid-1960s. Even after then, older generations would have taken offense.

Emerging in the 1960s, the Black Power movement supported rights and political power for the part of the American population that had been called over the years Negroes or colored, as well as many other derogatory names. In 1966, a militant political organization called the Black Panthers grew out of Oakland, California. James Brown's classic funk track *Say It Loud – I'm Black and I'm Proud* was released in 1968; it wasn't exactly poetry, but it expressed the developing mood and idiom of the times. In 1971, the Congressional Black Caucus provided a kind of official stamp of approval for the word. There might have been uncertainty about whether whites were entitled to use it, but that was soon clarified. By the mid-1970s, it was the only respectful way to refer to people of African heritage. African American didn't gain any traction in the popular lexicon until the 1980s, though the origins of the term go back to the earliest days of independence in the late eighteenth century; in 1782 to be precise, according to Jennifer Schuessler, of the *New York Times*, writing in 2015.

So, the word black isn't really about skin color, or anything phenotypical (that's observable characteristics): it's retaliation. For two years from 1965, there were uprisings in

practically every American city where there was a black
population. The violence started in the Watts neighborhood
of Los Angeles and eventually subsided in Detroit, where
after 5 days, 43 people were dead, 342 injured and 7,000
National Guard and army troops had been pressed into service. In this context, black people used black as a form of
vengeance: in some eras, racists had used it as an expletive, as
in '*You black* ...' and whatever noun came into their heads.
So, in a sense, it offered itself as a word that turned meaning
inside-out. 'Black is beautiful' was one of the sayings of the
period – this wasn't just a pronouncement; it was advice on
how to think about yourself.

Black was no more a description of skin color than white.
It could be argued that one was a sarcastic response to the
other. After all, whiteness was originally a political invention.
As Lerone Bennett wrote in his *The Shaping of Black
America*: 'The first white colonists had no concept of themselves as *white* men ... The word *white*, with all its burden of
guilt and arrogance, did not come into common usage until
the latter part of the [seventeenth] century.'

White servitude was a precursor to the exploitation of
blacks: 'Before the invention of the Negro or the white man
or the words and concepts to describe them, the colonial
population consisted largely of a great mass of white and
black bondsmen, who occupied roughly the same economic
category and were treated with equal contempt by the lords
of the plantations and legislatures.' Aligning with the plant-
ocracy as 'white' meant unburdening themselves of the harsh-
est aspects of bondage.

Theodore W. Allen favored similar terminology in his
book *The Invention of the White Race* (1994), which pays
particular attention to the experiences of migrant Irish, once
victimized and disparaged as degenerate and not amenable to
civilizing influences, yet later transformed into defenders of

an exploitative order. The Irish were certainly regarded by English colonizers as an inferior racial group (colonization of Ireland took place through the sixteenth century), but were physically indistinct from the English. There were other groups that would today be recognized as white that were readily associated with savagery. But, it became expedient to co-opt them.

History and exposition are often handy correctives. But they seem to have been drowned out by the deafening screech of abuse against Dolezal. It took the best part of a century before British colonizers created the inclusive label white (the first British slave settlement was established in Jamestown, Virginia, in 1607) and another 360 years before black came into being — at least in the way we understand and use it now. And nearly a half-century after that, people had either forgotten or never knew both terms are human artifices, not natural qualities. It's like building the pyramids as tombs for the pharaohs 4,000 years ago, then returning after a cryo-genically induced sleep, and assuming aliens put them there.

———————————————

Before we had the words biracial, mixed-race, half-caste or other neologisms that purport to describe accurately a person's genetic heritage, there was the one-drop rule. It stated that any person with even one ancestor of sub-Saharan-African ances-try, that is, with just one drop of African blood, is considered a Negro. The rule has no biological or genealogical founda-tion, though, in 1910, when Tennessee enshrined the rule in law, it was popularly regarded as having scientific status, how-ever spurious. By 1925, almost every state in America had some form of one-drop rule on its statute books. This was four decades before civil rights. Jim Crow segregation was in full force. Anti-miscegenation laws that prohibited unions of people considered to be of different racial types, remained until 1967, when the Supreme Court repealed them completely (*Loving v Virginia* 388 U.S. 1 (1967) was the relevant case).

Halle Berry has an African American father and a white mother, who was from Liverpool. Her parents divorced and she was brought up by her mother in Cleveland, Ohio. She had declared she considered herself biracial, this referring to a child with a black parent and a white parent: 'I do identify with my white heritage. I was raised by my white mother and every day of my life I have always been aware of the fact that I am biracial.'

Hardly a controversial figure, Berry had occasionally talked about the particular predicament of biracial people, but had never made an issue of it. At various points, she had also used black, African American and woman of color to describe herself. She had, in measured terms, talked of how she never felt accepted as white, despite her white mother. But her appeal to the one-drop rule seemed a bit like a physicist trying to explain the movements of celestial bodies by citing astrology.

The one-drop rule comments, made by Berry in an interview with Ebony magazine in 2011, came amidst a custody battle with her ex-partner, Gabriel Aubry, regarding their then two-year-old daughter, Nahla. (In 2014 Berry and Aubry were back in court regarding their daughter's hairstyle, a clash that was interpreted as centering around issues of race). And yet, with a sleight of argument, Berry contradictorily turned her anachronistic argument into one of the clearest statements on the race issue of recent years.

While it seemed irrational, Berry's explanation of her action in invoking the one-drop rule was far removed from any kind of faux biology or pseudoscience. 'I'm black and I'm her [daughter's] mother, and I believe in the one-drop theory. I'm not going to put a label on it. I had to decide for myself and that's what she's going to have to decide – how she identifies herself in the world,' she was quoted by Chloe Tilley, of the *BBC World Service*, in 2011.

In resisting conventional census categories, or labels, such as biracial or multiracial, she was not returning to another label *black*, as if returning to a default setting. Black, in her argument, is no longer a label; it is a *response* to a label — a response, that is, to not being white. Blackness, on this account, doesn't describe a color, a physical condition, a life-style, or even an ethnic status in the conventional sense: it is a reaction to being regarded as different or distinct. As the author and radio presenter Earl Ofari Hutchinson revealed in his 2011 article for *The Grio*, Berry and anyone who embraces this apparent paradox, 'effectively recognize the hard and unchanging reality that race relations and conflict in America are still framed in black and white.'

Black no longer describes a designated group of people: it's the way in which those who have been identified as distinct from and opposite to whites have reacted; their answer. When Berry allowed, 'that's what she's going to have to decide,' she meant that her daughter had some measure of discretion in the way she responds. Blackness is now a flex-ible and negotiable action; not the fixed status it once was. This doesn't mean blacks are no longer regarded as what phi-losophers call 'Other,' as definable objects, 'as those to be spoken for or about rather than with,' to use a suggestive phrase from the Australian scholar Juliana Mansvelt. Nor does it mean that the appropriation of cultural practices, images and artifacts such as downloads, movies and concerts are no longer predicated on blacks as continuously and unchangeably different. It means that blackness is not a thing, a category, a group or even a designation: it is, to repeat myself, a response to all of these.

The one-drop rule was an incongruous imposition on an otherwise sophisticated argument, an argument that carried added force, coming from someone not known for her out-spokenness or her humor. Berry had shown an awareness of history in 2002 when she dedicated her Oscar: 'This moment is so much bigger than me. This moment is for Dorothy Dandridge, Lena Horne, Diahann Carroll. This is for every faceless woman of color who now has a chance tonight because this door has been opened.' Dandridge (1922–1965), Horne (1917–2010) and Carroll (1935–) were all prominent African American entertainers, who, on reflection, may not have received the accolades they deserved. In 2017, Berry changed her mind when she declared her Oscar win 'meant nothing' citing the absence of 'people of color writing, directing, producing' as a persistent problem in the film industry.

A contemptuous shrug of dismissal might have been one kind of response to Dolezal. 'The woman identifies with and wishes to be regarded as black; so what?' And the retort would be something like: being black means belonging to a struggle that has been incubating for over four centuries and forms an indelible part of human history. It involves the enslavement, exploitation and oppression of about 12 million Africans and their offspring and, over time, the successive generations of people who have endured persecution, lynch-ing and brutality. Were this consigned to history, the inglori-ous episode would be terrible enough. But the narrative continues in different guises to the present day, with the des-cendants of slaves habitually mistreated. The bedeviling prac-tice of racism continues to motivate and justify the mistreatment of black people and identifying as black impli-cates a person in a daily conflict.

Has Dolezal been part of this conflict? No one actually asked the question, but I conjecture this is what was on many people's minds when they objected to Dolezal's self-description as black. Something similar might have been on

Germaine Greer's mind when she made her remark, 'Just because you lop off your dick and then wear a dress doesn't make you a fucking woman.' She was alluding to women's history of being denied the right to own property, vote, keep their own income, be educated, serve in the military, or in politics or participate in dozens of other pursuits that men have controlled. Feminists remain divided over transgendered women. 'Anyone born a man retains male privilege in society; even if he chooses to live as a woman,' is how Michelle Goldberg of *The New Yorker* sums up one position, presumably the one Greer would adopt. Women haven't been gifted their rights; they've fought for them. And this is where the debates intersect with the Dolezal controversy: had Dolezal paid her dues?

Kim Kardashian's genius is her primitivism. I mean her clear understanding of the value of what's simple, uncomplicated, though not necessarily unchallenging. She expresses this through her performance – some might call it art. So when she posed for the 2017 September issue of *Interview* magazine in clothes that looked like they could have been made by Jackie Onassis-Kennedy's personal designer Oleg Cassini, she knew there would be a spirited reaction. If readers hadn't quite grasped the comparison with Jackie, the magazine proclaimed Kim as 'America's New First Lady.' That was reason enough to make some readers scream in fury. After all, the much-loved Jackie O was synonymous with elegance, dignity and class. Kim is not typically associated with these qualities. Some suspected that Kardashian's skin had been digitally changed to look darker in the photos and to match the tone of her then four-year-old daughter, North, whose father is Kanye West. The Kardashians' ethnic heritage is Armenian, as well as English, Scottish, Irish, German and Dutch. North would have qualified as biracial under America's taxonomy (and that's how Halle Berry described herself on occasion, remember).

Earlier in the year, Kardashian had released promotional images, again looking curiously dusky, for her makeup line, KKW Beauty, though then she seemed more conciliatory in her response to criticism. 'I would obviously never want to offend anyone,' she told the *New York Times*. 'I used an amazing photographer and a team of people. I was really tan when we shot the images, and it might be that the contrast was off.' One twitter user wrote: 'Ugh she's a horrible person using cultural appropriation and not speaking about real issues.' Another tweeted: 'You black now sis?'

Black women and men, as I noted earlier, have lightened or, at least, been assumed to have lightened their skin for a variety of reasons. But not many apart from Kardashian have been slated for the opposite process — skin-*darkening*. Over the years, white actors have played black subjects, though the cultural context has usually permitted this. Laurence Olivier famously blacked-up in Stuart Burge's 1965 film version of *Othello*. Charlton Heston was heavily tinted for his role as a Mexican narcotics officer in Orson Welles' 1958 film *Touch of Evil*. There were no uproars, though few producers or directors would contemplate casting white actors in these roles today.

More recently, Zoë Saldana, whose mother is Puerto Rican and father from the Dominican Republic, darkened her skin for the part of Nina Simone in Cynthia Mort's biopic *Nina*, in 2016. 'It doesn't matter how much backlash I will get for it. I will honor and respect my black community because that's who I am,' Saldana told Judy Bachrach, of *Allure* magazine in 2013, adding, 'if Elizabeth Taylor can be Cleopatra, I can be Nina.'

Kardashian's digitized or perhaps cosmetic pigmentation adjustment was not for a film part, nor indeed any kind of part; but it *was* a performance. It was Kardashian shadow-playing Kardashian playing us. This was her way of entertaining, as if poking audiences with an electrified cattle-prod. Experience must have taught her that race issues don't coax her audience into a cozy slumber; they animate people into frenzy. In 2013 (and possibly earlier), she wore her hair in Fulani braids, as they're called (Fulani refers to a nomadic people in a region of West Africa; the women wear their hair in long braids hanging or looped on the sides). She wasn't the first Western woman to have worn her hair this way for the purposes of spectacle. The white actor Bo Derek produced no controversy at all when she wore her hair in the same style for the Blake Edwards movie *10*. This was released in 1979, a time when the word *black* was in everyday use, though not the term *cultural appropriation*.

Reverence was never Kardashian's strong point, so her homage to Jean-Paul Goude, the photographer, illustrator and author of the 1982 book, *Jungle Fever*, was never likely to be respectful, less still humble. This was actually a good thing: Goude's work was intended to inspire outrage rather than respect. Goude was an art director in the 1960s, later becoming partner and image consultant of Grace Jones. He designed the cover for Jones' *Island Life* (the one where she's in arabesque). The book was full of similar poses, including one called 'Carolina Beaumont, New York,' which depicts a naked black woman, her hair in a foot-high topknot, balancing a champagne coupe (a shallow saucer that was popular before flutes) on her protruding backside. She's popping the champagne so that the spume is arcing over her head into the glass. Goude's collection was not roundly criticized in the 1980s, though the image did recall nineteenth-century illustrations of Saartjie (sometimes, Sarah) Baartman, aka the Hottentot Venus, an African woman who was exhibited around Europe. The title of Goude's book conveyed his own taste – as he explained to *People's* Leo Wholfert in 1979: "I had jungle fever.'" He wasn't referring to a severe form of malaria.

Thirty-two years after Goude's book, Kardashian caricatured – that's surely the right word – his collection, many items of which were themselves caricatures. *PAPER* magazine made no attempt to conceal the intentions; the story bore the title 'Break the Internet Kim Kardashian' (Winter 2014). The Carolina Beaumont shot was changed so that Kardashian wore a pearl choker, satin evening gloves and a full-length black, beaded gown. Otherwise, the replication was close. She even wore the extended topknot. Other photographs included Kardashian, her body anointed in oil, baring her behind. The comparisons with Madonna's *SEX*, which I covered in Chapter 2, are inescapable: this was an entertainer, already established as one the world's most compelling women, who banked $52.5 million pre-tax between June 2014 and June 2015 (according to *Forbes'* Natalie Robehmed, March 8, 2016), taking off her clothes for public consumption.

Kardashian's genius, as I wrote, is primitivism: she believes in the value of simple behavior that's not always guided by logic or good sense. If it seems right to her, she does it. So playing with fire is not necessarily prohibited. There's no denying that she and her advisers have been able to convert this exceptional skill into an equally exceptional commercial enterprise. But often the money-making aspects of the Kardashian enterprise conceals the gift she has for playing with subjects that are deadly serious, but without getting hurt.

Race is a subject enshrouded in taboos; it's so germane to the American experience that caution is not enough: restraint, kid-glove carefulness and an observance of others' sensibilities are recommended when approaching. In a sense, America's history, before and after the 1775–1783 revolution, is pockmarked by racism. It's been one of the nation's most disfiguring problems. Yet Kardashian seemed to treat a humungous social issue with the glibness of a soap opera subplot. As well as the hairdos and the skin darkening, she also wore grills, which are ornamental metal covers for the teeth, usually associated with hip-hop culture. In fairness, many whites have worn grills, including Katy Perry and Cara Delevingne. But there seemed deliberateness about Kardashian's habit of adopting styles and affectations that were likely to provoke resentment. In 2018, she showed off her silver-dyed Fulani braids via a series of selfies shared through Snapchat. The riposte was predictably hostile. 'Kim Kardashian should have learned by now how to properly deal with black culture and considering she has three black kids this behavior is disturbing,' stated one post.

It's precisely that last point that presumably makes Kardashian feel entitled to collide with indignant fans (and antagonists) who complain she thieves like a magpie from black culture. Kardashian would presumably plead innocent to 'the unconscionable crime of appropriating blackness,' as Daniel Harris called Dolezal's offense (considered earlier in this chapter). In 2012, Kardashian started seeing Kanye West, then ranked number 10 in *Billboard*'s top R&B/hip-hop artists (he is no longer included in the magazine's top 50 artists of the genre). They married in Florence in May 2014. By that time, the couple had their first baby, North. West was Kardashian's third husband. Her first was Damon Thomas, like West an African American. Her second was Kris Humphries, the basketball player; he's white.

West didn't claim to be an advocate of civil rights though, on occasion, he did strive to use his position to speak to the nation above the crossfire. For example, in 2005, in a charity telethon for Hurricane Katrina's victims, he memorably told viewers: 'George Bush doesn't care about black people.' It was a reference to the apparent indifference of the then US President to the plight of those who were suffering in the wake of the flood in New Orleans. A disproportionate number of those affected were African Americans. Bush himself fumed: 'It's one thing [for Kanye West] to say, you know, that I don't appreciate the way that he's handled his business. It's another thing to say that this man's a racist. I resent it, it's not true, and it's one of the most disgusting moments of my presidency.'

West's comment seemed relatively innocuous in the context of popular music, much of which is critical of the political mainstream, though tracks such as Public Enemy's *Fight the Power*, released in 1989, and NWA's *Fuck tha Police*, in 1988, seemed like echoes from a distant age. Rappers were not supposed to think too critically about social events any more, and, if they did, they were supposed to keep their thoughts to themselves. When the rapper 50 Cent criticized West for his statement, it seemed to signal how discouragingly placid the once raging hip-hop culture had become.

The seven words did West's career no harm at all. At a time when most artists were preservationists when it came to their own careers, a little anarchistic intrusion was a relief, especially on live TV. All the same, West showed contrition five years later: 'I would tell George Bush, in my moment of frustration, I didn't have the grounds to call him a racist,' said West. His only other brush with controversy came in 2009 when he leapt onstage at the MTV Music Awards and interrupted the then 19-year-old Taylor Swift during her acceptance speech for Best Female Video. 'Beyoncé had one of the best videos of all time,' he interjected (the Beyoncé track in question was *Single Ladies (Put a Ring On It)*). While

West didn't say or even imply Swift's award reflected a racist bias, he later alluded to this, though confusingly, when, in a radio interview, he said: 'It's not about Kanye West. It's not about Taylor Swift ... There's a lot of people in America that feel like they don't have the platform to stand up and express their closet racism.' Exactly what he meant remains unclear. 'Closet racism' is not a popular term, though its source is obviously 'closet homosexuality,' which means unacknowledged or secretive. I confess I don't know where to start, not understanding what he meant.

There is a breath of authenticity about West's occasional outbursts. He is alive, sentient and an African American. Kardashian's, however, are ambiguous. Her robust defense of YouTube makeup vlogger Jeffree Star, for example, had an almost comic flavor. Star posted a tweet criticizing Kardashian's makeup. 'Kim what is going on with those new swatches?' he tweeted. 'Looks like chalk' (when someone tries out makeup, then posts pictures online, the pictures are called 'swatches.') Kardashians' supporters took angrily to their keyboards. While Star's comments didn't seem racist, he did have some previous form and, at one point, faced a boycott from black consumers.

Kardashian didn't mind his comments and posted an online video in which she excused Star: 'I see you being so petty bringing up things in his past where he was negative, but he's also apologized for those things. I get it's a serious deal if you say racial things, but I do believe in people changing and people that apologize I will give them the benefit of the doubt and accept that people change and move on.'

Perhaps the ambiguity is what makes Kardashian's interventions so curious. Married to an African American with children, who may or may not identify as black (if we accept Halle Berry's point), herself of mixed ethnic heritage,

Kardashian never shrinks from an issue that's as safe as an unexploded bomb.

'This week we watched Alton Sterling and Philando Castile two innocent black men, get senselessly murdered by police officers,' wrote Kardashian on her website and app in July 2016, using the hashtag #BlackLivesMatter. 'I do not ever want to have to teach my son to be scared of the police, or tell him that he has to watch his back because the people we are told to trust – the people who "protect and serve" – may not be protecting and serving him because of the color of his skin.'

Castile and Sterling were two African American men shot and killed by US police officers in July 2016. Their deaths were the 504th and 505th killings respectively by police up to that point in the year. Of those killed, 24 per cent were black. Blacks make up 13.3 per cent of the American population. Both Castile and Sterling had their final moments caught on camera and, because of this, their deaths were watched by millions across the world. They were far from isolated cases. The deaths were met with the anger that had been building since 2012, when the fatal shooting of 17-year-old African American Trayvon Martin by George Zimmerman, a neighborhood watch volunteer, enlivened debates about the manner in which police treated blacks. While Martin wasn't shot by police, Zimmerman was acquitted, prompting three activists – Alicia Garza, Opal Tometi and Patrisse Cullors – to create the hashtag #BlackLivesMatter in protest. This was the movement referred to by Kardashian in her post.

Much of the response to the protest was predictable: as if the deaths were isolated cases in which things went grotesquely wrong rather than pieces of a larger sequence of events that stretched back decades, if not centuries. The 2014 killing of Michael Brown, an unarmed teenager who was walking with a friend in Ferguson, St Louis, seemed to typify the experience: a white Ferguson police officer shot him. Six times. A Department of Justice investigation ultimately determined the officer didn't violate Brown's civil rights.

Only naive people would assume the deaths were something new and unexpected: the Rodney King beating at the hands of LAPD officers during his arrest in 1991 fits into the succession, as do the many events leading to the upheavals in Watts in 1965. The difference between these and earlier instances of police brutality on blacks is that Web 2.0 wasn't around. It sounds facile to suggest a piece of technology was responsible for a kind of cultural awakening that led to #BlackLivesMatter but it wasn't the technology itself that made the difference: it was how people decided to use it to dispense information, share stories and offer advice on how best to make feelings known. The parallels with #MeToo are obvious: the web has the potential to draw dissimilar people, with distinct backgrounds, contrasting politics and disparate lives into harmony over one big issue. The battle for justice was fought as never before – digitally.

While Kardashian's excited show of concern wouldn't necessarily qualify her as an activist, it did align her with many other celebrities who had used #BlackLivesMatter to express their opinions and stave off those who criticized them for doing so. Actor Jesse Williams wrote: 'If you have no interest in equal rights for black people, then do not make suggestions to those who do.' Among the many others who supported #BlackLivesMatter were Kerry Washington, John Legend, Mark Zuckerberg and The Weeknd, though it was left to an athlete to take one further step and demonstrate his belief, not just in the # but in the meaning of the words.

Colin Kaepernick's silent protest began in 2016, when he started kneeling during the American national anthem preceding National Football League (NFL) games. The player wanted to call attention to the seemingly perpetual police brutality, but his gesture mushroomed into a social movement that drew world attention to America's racial divide. Kaepernick roiled powerful institutions from the NFL to the White House, and forced everyone to wrestle with difficult questions about protest, patriotism and free speech, as well as racism.

Paradoxically, it was Donald Trump who gave impetus to Kaepernick's resistance movement. 'Wouldn't you love to see one of these NFL owners, when somebody disrespects our flag, to say, "Get that son of a bitch off the field right now?"' asked the then President at a political rally in Alabama. It delighted Trump's white conservative constituency of support, but horrified many others, especially the thousands of black athletes, not only in the NFL but other sports. (According to an HBO/Marist poll, 47 per cent of Americans thought athletes should be required to stand during the anthem against 51 per cent who maintained no rule should exist.)

Much of American sports is a theater in which black people exhibit their skills and physical prowess for the delectation of fans, the majority of which are white. Over 200 athletes refused to stand following Trump's comment.

Several showbusiness entertainers stuck up for Kaepernick. Jay Z, for example, wore a Kaepernick jersey on TV. The rapper Common also aligned himself: 'Man, I don't know how your country would think that talking about equality is wrong.' Stevie Wonder dropped to his knees before a concert and said: 'Tonight, I'm taking a knee for America.'

Kaepernick had worn socks with images of police officers dressed as pigs; he'd also refused to vote at the 2016 presidential election. So he was a challenging rather than popular character. He was probably aware that he'd have as much backlash as any athlete since John Carlos and Tommie Smith, whose black power salute at the 1968 Olympics provoked an even more volatile reaction. Like Muhammad Ali before them, they were suspended from competition. Ali had refused the military draft in 1967 and was stripped of his title. At the start of the 2018–2019 season, Kaepernick did not have a club and was effectively unemployed. The NFL had no African American owners.

Despite being reviled by Trump and many others, Kaepernick was awarded Ambassador of Conscience by Amnesty International. In his acceptance speech in April 2018, Kaepernick described police killings of African Americans as lawful lynching: 'Racialized oppression and dehumanization is woven into the very fabric of our nation – the effects of which can be seen in the lawful lynching of black and brown people by the police.'

In 1955, James Baldwin closed his book *Notes of a Native Son* with the reminder: 'This world is white no longer, and it will never be white again.' The legislation intended to end segregation in public places and banish discrimination on the basis of 'race, color, religion, sex or national origin' was still nine years away.

In 1997, the historian Paul Spickard reflected that, since the 1960s, America had experienced: 'A modest softening of the lines between the races.' Apart from the word 'race' to describe cultural groups, it seemed an unexceptional statement: more than three decades after civil rights, some abatement of the strife and divisions that marked America's prehistory would have been expected. Spickard then added: 'This is not to suggest that race is becoming less important in American public life – on the contrary, it continues to shape people's life chances far more drastically than white conservative rhetoric would have us believe.'

Some scholars think America has just been reinventing the wheel since the 1960s, spending a great deal of effort and doing much handwringing but without ever closing a cultural fissure that has been, in many senses, the nation's dominant feature. Writing in the *Journal of Negro Education*, Dirk Philipsen, offered this persuasive thought: 'The entire spectrum of life experiences by Americans not only are perceived, but also processed and acted upon in a way that is pervasively racialized.' By racialized, I take it that Philipsen meant treated in a way made comprehensible in terms of race. If this doesn't surprise us quite as much it should in the twenty-first century, why is that?

Perhaps because it resembles commonsense: a glance at the patterns of inequality can be rendered intelligible in terms of either a mutant racism that's adapted to changing environments and continues to exert maleficent influence, *or* as an expression of some races' inability or perhaps unwillingness to improve their material positions. The latter seems a more popular option. But it's inconsistent with the way life is changing in the twenty-first century. To maintain a race-prone position in an environment of fluidity and amorphousness (by which I mean without a fixed shape) seems oddly old-fashioned, if not downright regressive. But it explains why Rachel Dolezal met with such fury. It seemed she had somehow insulted a biologically distinct and homogenous subspecies of humankind with common features, a shared culture, language and history — a race.

For reasons I've explained, the first part of this conception of race is spurious. The second part — about culture, language and history — is reason enough to prompt questions of Dolezal, but, in this writer's opinion at least, not enough to disqualify her from identifying as black. No more than it would stop Halle Berry's daughter from calling herself white and conducting her life as a white person. This would be no masquerade, just a sign of the times. If we dare to sneer at the male-female binary, why do we respect the racial equivalent? A shared history is a potent force but, when used to resist reason, it acts like an antibody counteracting change. Resisting a more fluid approach to blackness seems to me to be playing with rules that were established long ago by people who decided to call themselves white and, for political and economic reasons, wanted to perpetuate the falsehood that they belonged to an exclusive and distinguishable category.

What about whites today? Matthew W. Hughey reckons whiteness is now 'less of a synonym for invisible normality' than it was just a few years ago. And, when Toni Bruce argues, 'the instability of dominant discourses means that the boundaries of the "normal" must be constantly marked,' she implies there is more transience than we typically assume. Hundreds of years of conceiving people as black leaves an impression of permanence. A genuinely fluid culture would change this.

As I've argued, the term black would be meaningless: both blackness and whiteness would be dispatched to oblivion. This won't happen. More likely we will witness the kind of situation encouraged by Halle Berry, in which ethnicity becomes a matter of choice, people electing their ethnic identities. Note the use of plural *identities*: Berry's child may change hers as she grows, perhaps opting for several at one time, changing to suit different situations. It will be – probably already is – possible to have multiple ethnicities, all interchangeable and all fluid.

For some, this lack of certainty must sound like a waking nightmare. Surely we can't change identities and switch ethnicities as we change our appearance with cosmetic surgery, replace limbs with prosthetics, restore vital functions with organ transplants from human donors or realign our sex with how we think about ourselves. But that's what is happening and, for this writer at least, it is no bad thing. If this means the disappearance of blackness, then so be it.

James Baldwin was before his time with his 'white no longer' salutation in 1955. He would still be too early if he said it today. But tomorrow, he will be right: the death of blackness will bring with it the demise of whiteness and all the inequity, oppression, bigotry and manifold wrongdoing that malefactor has engendered.

CHAPTER 5

INFLUENTIAL PRESENCE

'Audiences will flock to this for two reasons – either they want to see Paris Hilton in her undies, or they want to see her horribly killed,' wrote Helen O'Hara, of *Empire*, the film magazine. She was reviewing *House of Wax* (2005), 'a movie whose biggest draw is profoundly untalented hotel-fortune heiress Paris Hilton,' as Maitland McDonah, of *TV Guide*, put it – awarding the film ★★. The *Guardian*'s Peter Bradshaw was no more enthusiastic: 'This horror film about inert wax dummies who look like dead people stars … Paris Hilton. Ahem.'

Hilton's foray into music, in 2006, met with slightly more warmth: 'She sings like a woman who has heard of something called singing, can't be sure of exactly what it might entail, but is fairly certain you do something a bit like this,' wrote Alexis Petridis of the album *Paris*.

Her 2004 book, *Confessions of an Heiress: A Tongue-in-Chic Peek Behind the Pose* made the *Telegraph*'s Top Ten Worst Celebrity Books. But not the worst sellers; it shifted over a million copies worldwide and amply justified the reputed $100,000 advance royalty. 'Which just goes to show you don't have to know a lot about anything to write a little about something,' concluded Shirley Halperin, of *The Hollywood Reporter*.

The thing about Paris Hilton is: she wasn't easily deterred. The opinions of reviewers, critics and other arbiters of taste were of secondary importance. What audiences wanted was her priority. And what they appeared to want more than anything was to look, smell and behave like her. Whether she was taking selfies, carrying a Hermès tote, or stroking her Chihuahua, people mimicked her, suggesting that, somehow, she'd acquired a facility for affecting how people act. She was an unwitting exemplar 'setting not only every fashion and lifestyle trend at the time,' as Emilia Petrarca, of *W*, put it, 'but also defining what it meant to be an "influencer" before we even had a word for it.' What's more, she figured out a way of making her influence pay.

In 2000, Hilton, then 19, signed with T Models, a New York City-based modeling agency owned by Donald Trump (and later known as Trump Model Management; it closed in 2017). As part of the hotel-owning Hiltons, she was already wealthy and lived extravagantly; she also enjoyed the company of recognizable men. But she lacked one thing that in the early twenty-first century was even more valuable than money: fame. It appears she had no specific career strand in mind beyond becoming famous. Her reputation as an 'It girl' — a young woman who achieves fame because of her socialite lifestyle — was clearly not enough. Happily for her, she was around when not being able to sing, dance or act was no impediment; in fact, it gave Hilton license to move into any sphere of activity she pleased. Her shortage of ortho- dox skills made this movement frictionless. In place of talent, Hilton offered presence. Some might call it aura or charisma, but, in her case, it really was just presence. She appeared.

Context was always crucial; time, place, others present and events preceding and following make actions speak louder than words. So when, in November 2003, a four-minute video featuring Hilton engaging in sex with her one-time boyfriend Rick Salomon began circulating online, it made Hilton infamous. Describing the transition as friction-less, in this instance, may not be quite right. Hilton sued and was awarded $400,000; she claimed she never intended the video to be a commercial venture and in later interviews said the release of the tape felt like rape. But the timing of the leak, it could be argued, did have some benefits, coming, as it did, three weeks before the launch of a reality TV show called *The Simple Life*, in which Hilton and her then-friend Nicole Richie incongruously did menial jobs on a farm. Any student of Madonna would have known that the sex tape scandal practically assured stellar ratings for the show. (The internet wasn't around when Madonna essayed notoriety with impious videos and risqué books, but it's a safe bet that, if it had been, she would have used it to her advantage.)

By late 2003, Paris Hilton had accrued some of the valu-able resource she evidently craved. Her name was known glo-bally and the kind of offers attendant on fame were abundant. The ghost-written (by Merle Ginsberg) *Confessions of an Heiress* was Hilton's literary debut and it became a best-seller, despite a mauling by critics. After a few minor appearances in films, she went to Australia to make *House of Wax*. Again, the critics' derision wasn't matched by the audience response; it cost $30 million to make and grossed $70 million at the box office.

Hilton may have added novelty value, but it was still *value*. Hilton was clearly aspirational, but her aspiration was undefined. An album, a gig as a DJ, a range of fragrances, another reality TV series, and a spell in jail (she served 23 days in 2007 for a probation violation after a driving offense), all performed with an imperious disregard for conventionally defined talent, supported Newton's Third Law – for every *action*, there is an equal and opposite reaction. Critical slating → consumer expenditure.

As Lola Ogunnaike, of the *New York Times*, declared in 2005: 'Ms. Hilton may not come across as the sharpest knife in the drawer, but she is a Mensa-caliber genius at being a celebrity.' Seeming to be simultaneously naïve and sagacious, illiterate and erudite, devoid of talent and touched by genius, Hilton was arguably the first celebrity to *monetize* presence. A spot of illicit sex set her celebrity career in motion perhaps, but unlike countless other provisional celebrities who found fame fleeting and then irretrievable, Hilton decided to turn ubiquity into money. She signed with Endeavor, the Hollywood talent agency, changed publicity houses, defecting from PMK/HBH to Dan Klores Communications, but stuck with Trump's model agency. Her tie-up with Parlux Fragrances proved fruitful and she expanded into cosmetics.

By 2018, there were 24 Paris Hilton fragrances on the market. Following in the footsteps of Elizabeth Taylor, who pioneered celebrity fragrances in the 1980s, Hilton diversified into jewelry. She also lent her name to handbags, energy drinks and miscellaneous products pitched at the cheaper end of the market. In 2005, Fred Khalilian, a Florida-based businessman who made his fortune in the fitness world, reportedly paid Hilton a seven-figure sum to join forces in opening a string of clubs.

Ogunnaike relates a story of how Hilton, when shopping at Patricia Field, in Manhattan, contemplated buying a $1,000 pair of pumps. 'You all should give these to me for free,' Hilton told the three salespeople in attendance. 'Once I wear them, you know that they are going to be in all the magazines and everyone is going to write about them.' The staff clearly understood the logic of her proposition and gave her the shoes for free.

Readers will have realized I am not merely trying to rehabilitate the popular Hilton image as vacuous-blonde-with-Chihuahua. It might work with people who don't examine the way she engineered a multi-purpose machine to make money. 'If you want to make fun of yourself and play into the whole stereotype, then why not?' she was quoted in Ogunnaike's story. 'Obviously I know what I'm doing.' Well, perhaps not *obviously*. After all, she uttered lines such as, 'Walmart? What's that? Do they like make walls there?'

She was probably playing to the crowd, intent on sustaining an image that would become her most valuable possession. 'Where would I be,' she must have wondered, 'without an audience that loves to make fun of me?' Hilton capitalized on her fame, which might have been as short-lived as the many other reality show celebs that emerged in the first decade of the century. She knew she was watchable and this meant people would pay to watch her. And if they paid to watch her, whether on film or in the flesh, they might pay to possess products associated with her image, or even just her name. That's what I meant earlier when I wrote Hilton offered presence. At a price.

Influencer n. *person with the capacity to influence the behavior or opinions of others, esp. in purchasing of goods and services; one who seeks to influence others' consumption habits on social media for money.*

Stephen Brown, a professor of marketing, in a 2015 article in *Arts Marketing*, recalls an apocryphal story about Pablo Picasso (1881–1973). A visitor to the master's Parisian studio stared perplexedly at one of his typically frenzied canvases. 'What does it represent?' enquired the visitor, to which

Picasso shot back, 'About twenty thousand dollars.' Brown's point is that there is a myth about some artists and performers remaining 'uncontaminated' while others abase themselves by pursuing commercial gain. Even the greats don't consider money an adulteration.

So, when actor Jon Hamm pronounced in 2012, 'Whether it's Paris Hilton or Kim Kardashian or whoever, stupidity is certainly celebrated ... Being a fucking idiot is a valuable commodity in this culture,' he was presumably aggrieved that people who didn't ply a traditional trade in the entertainment industry, were, as he correctly stated, valuable commodities. And Jason Statham, when asked whether he considered his name and image a brand, retorted, 'No ... Kim Kardashian's a brand.' Hamm advertised H&R Block accountants at the time. Statham advertised LG phones.

When anybody, actor, artist or artisan, criticizes today's indeterminately talented celebrities for setting their sights solely on mammon, they start from a position of weakness. Audiences decide who has talent and influence. There's no absolute standard that's good for all ages across all territories. Influence, in particular, reveals itself in sales. And that is exactly what Paris Hilton must have realized early in her fledgling celebrity career: that the only advantage you take from not having obvious talent is that you can turn *yourself* into the commodity you're intending to sell. No one is going to be distracted by questions like, 'Where do I know her from?' 'What does she do in her day job?' or 'Why should I take her word for it?' Hilton just appeared in her quintessential role as Paris Hilton and asked nothing more of her audience than their awareness of her.

Celebrity culture has its own prehistory: it started in the 1960s when Liz Taylor outraged and horrified people with her imagined violation of propriety and morality; her affairs – at first with Eddie Fisher and, later and more epically, with Richard Burton — scandalized the world and induced the media to take a more proactive approach to reporting the lives of the famous — and us to take a more prurient interest in their private lives. The media and we waited till the 1980s before Madonna arrived with her try-anything-to-get-a-reaction approach. There was method in Madonna's apparent mayhem; she offered something that seemed forbidden but relieved audiences of any guilt they might have had for snooping on her private life. After Madonna, audiences became accustomed to the taboo delights she offered. They and their proxy, the media, became more intrusive, as they adjusted to a new morality; one in which the line between private and public domains was getting fuzzy.

Audiences were like ravening wolves when Paris Hilton arrived. But there was no interest in someone who hadn't offered at least a pretext for watching or listening. She was just another rich kid. This is why Hilton is what anthropologists call a 'liminal being': an ambiguous figure who defies easy categorization. The commodity she peddled was Paris Hilton, a name, an image and an evocation of practically anything. She was empty and expressionless to the point that audiences had to imagine. But today, that's what we do: we don't actually know celebrities. We think we know them and have ways of keeping our assumed knowledge up to date.

Had Hilton surfaced in, let's say, 1993 (10 years before the sex tape was uploaded), the internet would have been in its infancy, MTV's *The Real World* (or *Real World*, as it became) would have been the only reality TV show, and Nokia would have been six years away from introducing the first portable phone that could fit in the palm of a hand (model 3210). *The Simple Life* was one of several shows that had been spawned, however indirectly, by *Big Brother*, which was launched by CBS in the USA in 2000 (it started in the

Netherlands in 1999) and exposed the public appetite for voyeurism. Over 2004 and 2005, Web 2.0 provided the internet with a facility we now take for granted: interactivity. Users were no longer consumers of information; they also created and shared content. When Facebook launched on the unpromising premise that people liked exchanging purposeless information via their computers, it didn't seem to have a hope of success. It entered people's hearts and minds so quickly that, by the time Hilton served her spell in prison (2007), people must have been wondering how on earth they survived without it (it had 50 million followers by October 2007; there are about 2.2 billion active users now).

In 2007, Apple introduced its iPhone (with OSX), a device that allowed watching films, listening to music and browsing the internet as well has having a 2 mega-pixel camera; by 2017, 1.2 trillion digital photographs per year were being taken, 85 per cent on phones. For a period in the early 2000s, Hilton must have been the most photographed figure in the world; armed with cameras in their phones, people snapped her practically everywhere she went: shops, gyms, bars, restaurants, walking, getting in and out of cars. It's impossible to think of anyone else whose everyday movements have been subject to comparable surveillance. Without this and, of course, the gossip that gingered up the images, Paris Hilton, the public entity, wouldn't have existed. And, when I say public entity, I mean there were thousands, perhaps millions of Hiltons that lived beyond time and space – they were in her audience's imagination.

The marketing possibilities of such a being evidently didn't escape Hilton. Whereas celebrities had previously lent their names, faces and imprimaturs to products as a way of endorsing them, Hilton *became* the product. She effectively put herself on the market to be bought and sold like any other piece of merchandise. Some might call this inherently tacky, while others call it brilliant. And some might call Hilton lucky, while others call her perspicacious. Perhaps not; but clear-sighted for sure. She saw the unprecedented gathering of media technologies that would allow her to be everywhere 24-hours a day, and how ubiquity could be monetized. Serendipity?

――――――――――――

The question not usually asked when analysts consider the most influential influencers or how influencers exercise their influence is this: *why* are they influential? Could it be something to do with *relatability*? This is one of those words that makes the people who dreamed up 'positivity' and 'narrativize' look like a bunch of amateurs, but, if treated with care, it might assist our understanding of the often puzzling relationships between celebrities and their devotees. People were able to feel they could relate to Hilton. At another time in history, she might have been disparaged as a 'rich bitch' with more money than sense and in need of an honest day's work. But, in the improvident 2000s when people sought endless novelty, bounteous glamor, lavishness in all areas of their lives and the arousal of their senses by whatever stimulant was ready-to-hand, Hilton was perfect.

Think of Hilton in the same way as a new toy. When gifted to a child, the child feels a thrill and plays excitedly with the new possession. She or he relates to the plaything. But only for as long as it takes for a new toy to arrive, then another and another. Then the first toy's value is lessened as if by a law of diminishing returns: each new toy depreciates the value of all the others until a kind of saturation point arrives. Then, the value of the toys resides not so much in the objects themselves, but in their novelty or newness. The newer, the better. (I've taken and modified this illustration from the literary critic Waldo Frank, 1889–1967.)

It could be argued that the fans discovered Hilton and decided she'd serve as a kind of distributor of taste, standard and values. She just happened to be conveniently in the right place at the right time. Others will insist the corporations that signed and projected Hilton as their emblem of conspicuous consumption manipulated consumers. Still others might suggest there was an elective affinity, that is, a correspondence with or feeling of attraction toward Hilton the person, her attitudes, and lifestyle. This is what I mean by *relatability*: Hilton didn't so much have it; others endowed her with it.

The ill-starred ventures into film and music were probably no more than bait: as a fisher tempts bigger catches with sprats, Hilton kept the media amused in the confident expectation that they'd react with snarky reviews. Her fans would be amused and she remained in the public discourse. The only thing she couldn't budget for was the relentless appetite for renewal: audiences became bored with her, as children become bored with their toys. Novelty, freshness, upgrades; Hilton's value shrank as every new celeb emerged to stake a claim on public attention.

Let me paint a picture. It's 2006 and Paris Hilton is under contract with Nicole Richie to make *The Simple Life*. The pair are no longer on affable terms and the show's makers feature them in separate episodes wherever possible. The simmering feud becomes a sort of backstory to the main narrative of the show, adding more interest. Hilton's by-now materializing grand plan requires her to maintain public appearances, especially at clubs and stores – her natural environments. Among her entourage, is an unknown friend who manages to squeeze into some of the thousands of photographs taken of Hilton and company every day. Camera-phones are now popularly available, though the epoch-making iPhone won't be on sale until next year.

Hilton's friend is four months older than she is and has been divorced since 2004 (she eloped and married at 19).

While the two friends don't have what you might describe as a purely business relationship, Hilton asks her to do jobs for her. For example, she charges her with the responsibility for organizing her wardrobe. It probably sounds a less onerous job than it actually is; Hilton's clothes racks are comparable with those of department stores and she likes them color-coded. Impressed with her work, Hilton invites her friend to become her personal stylist and accompany her on various assignments; she even lets her appear, albeit briefly, in some episodes of her reality show. In retrospect it might be surmised that Kardashian now has an opportunity to study Hilton close-up and analyze how she sustains her profile.

And then something happens that places a strain on their friendship. In early 2007, a 30-minute video featuring her friend *in flagrante* is released under the title *Kim Kardashian Superstar*. Four years before, a shorter but equally explicit video of Hilton effectively launched her career. Like Hilton, her friend, who is, of course, Kim Kardashian, takes legal action. She agrees to a settlement, reported to be $5 million, in May 2007. Two months later, she announces she will appear nude in *Playboy*. Hilton, who had been released from jail on June 26, having served 22 days, must be wondering whether Kardashian is her friend or apprentice. *The Simple Life* is axed in August. The December issue of *Playboy* features a revealing picture on the cover with the strap HOLLYWOOD'S NEW SEX STAR KIM KARDASHIAN TAKES IT ALL OFF.

Same epoch: change of characters. Kardashian's arrival in the public consciousness didn't signal the beginning of a new period in cultural history, or even a new phase of celebrity culture, though it did perhaps mark a subdivision of the era distinguished by Hilton. Kardashian was a new toy. I hope readers will have already read between my lines and realize

Hilton represented a new form of advertising. I don't mean this to sound cynical; there was creativity, design, ingenuity and a dollop of outrageousness in Hilton's enterprise. The circumstances, technology and social climate might have offered her a perfect low-pressure weather system, but she had to figure out a way of harnessing the storm to her own purposes; and the concept of monetizing yourself was inspired. Remember: previously, stars built reputations for their skills, prowess and accomplishments, then transferred these to the products they hawked. Hilton had nothing: she just appeared. And people paid for it.

Hilton had probably factored in the public's developing fascination with glitz, glamor, affluence, hedonism and the ethic of impulse over calculation. She might have worked out how the logic of consumerism governed the way the media depicted reality and how people were socialized to want a neverending supply of new commodities (and I'm using *socialized* to mean being taught to be social beings — society not only imposes patterns on our behavior, but reaches inside us to organize our thoughts and desires). She could even anticipate that the obsession with newness and change would precipitate her descent and her replacement by other, less familiar faces. It's possible she heard the skittering footsteps of Kardashian behind her. Yet, she had no magic to remake herself in the manner of Madonna, who kept interest in her alive by practically forcing audiences to imagine her anew every three or four years; 29 years after her Blond Ambition tour, Madonna announced her eleventh world tour, Madame X.

Much as celebrities and the commercial organizations behind them try to create new demands and new discontents that can only be assuaged by buying more new commodities, they're helpless to turn back time. So when the celebrity herself is the commodity, there is a self-obsolescing process that just can't be reversed.

_____

Overheard during a conversation at the Blue Bottle café, on West Sunset Boulevard, LA, in February 2007:

— Kardashian? What's that? One of those republics that used to be part of the Soviet Union? A new shampoo?

— *I'm serious; you should book this woman for the show. She's going to be bigger than big and everyone will be talking about her now that her sex tape has gone viral.*

— Sex tapes have been done before. Pam Anderson's tape took her to a new level, I grant you. But she could act: she was already a TV star on *Baywatch*.

— *But Paris Hilton wasn't. She didn't act, or even sing, dance or anything.*

— OK, but lightning doesn't strike twice. Advertisers always go to celebrity endorsers who are known for something else. Nicole Kidman had been in *Moulin Rouge* and a dozen other movies when she did the Chanel No. 5 commercials. JLo is doing this Live perfume, but she's a known commodity through her music. Paris made it big *because* she didn't have talent, not in spite of it. I know this Kardashian worked for her and knows all her moves, but she can't duplicate her. Paris is a one-off.

— *Or she could be a template.*

— Meaning?

— *Paris could serve as a new model for others to copy. She had nothing but … well, Paris. She sold herself as a package. And this new woman knows her tricks.*

– Look. My show is a talk show: we have guests who can talk about their new film, book, album or whatever they want to sell. What are we going to say about this Kardashian? What is she pitching?

– *This is where you're going to have to reorganize how you think: she's selling her image, name, even her initials. When her reality show starts, she'll be on everybody's mind and they'll all be talking about her and her family, just like they were Paris and Nicole Richie. And, I know this Kardashian woman; she is full of surprises: once she gets attention, it's like a drug to her – she'll keep shocking people until the whole world recognizes her and knows her name. Anyway, people always remember someone whose family name starts with a K.*

– Who told you that, Diane Keaton? Hah! Or Ben Kingsley?

– *Actually, you just reminded me when you mentioned Nicole Kidman.*

'The Kardashians are an inescapable cultural and commercial force,' observed Harriet Ryan and Adam Tschorn, of the *Los Angeles Times*, in 2010. *Keeping Up With the Kardashians* had just completed its fourth season on E! providing the cable network with its most viewed program ever. Kim's website was the most visited in history. 'And Madison Avenue calls on the [Kardashian] family to sell mainstream America, from diet pill and orange juice to NASCAR and fast food,' wrote Ryan and Tschorn, before musing: 'Their popularity comes despite the fact that the sisters lack the talents that tradition-ally lead to superstardom and, some believe, partly because of it.'

'Once Paris Hilton and Lindsay Lohan ruled the scene,' wrote Christine Kearney, of the *Ottawa Citizen*, in 2010. 'But these days, [Kim] Kardashian gets the wall-to-wall coverage ... has built herself into a brand.' Lohan was the child model and actor, who made a best-selling album, played Elizabeth Taylor in a TV movie and became a darling of the tabloids when she discovered and acquired a taste for drugs and alcohol. Scrapes with the law, a prison sentence and a rumored lesbian relationship kept her in focus, even while her official professional career decayed. Lohan held contracts to endorse handbags, self-tanning spray and leggings, but a 90-day sentence in rehab after lying to the police about driving during a car crash convinced some brands that she no longer possessed the right kind of influence. (Lohan had a highly publicized – and therefore, highly valuable – feud with Hilton.)

By 2010, Kim Kardashian, then 30, could lay claim to being the most influential woman in the world. Influential, that is, in shaping and steering consumer choices. Influencers can make things happen; they can change the order of the marketplace. No one supposes they are superior beings, their erudition, discernment and capability for appreciating style making them perfect tastemakers whom we should imitate respectfully. They just capture attention and incline us toward buying some products rather than others. And Kardashian did it with more authority than anybody, arguably, in history.

Kardashian's frontal assault on the public senses and her stealthier advance on their bank accounts continued in 2011: she got married on TV. And to a sports star. Brits do this kind of thing rather well, of course. Royal weddings typically spellbind TV-viewing populations from around the world (it was reported that 2 billion watched some part of the wedding of Prince William and Kate Middleton in 2011). E! had previously screened Kim's sister Khloé's wedding in 2009. So weddings were a new pipeline. Kim's wedding to Kris Humphries, a professional basketball player, was turned into hard cash by Kim's mother Kris Jenner, who, with a touch worthy of King Midas, negotiated deals for every aspect of the event, from the wedding gown by Vera Wang, to the crystal-embellished black-and-white engraved gatefold invitations by Lehr & Black, the custom invitation specialists.

About $500,000 will buy a full-page advertisement in a magazine like *Brides*, which has a circulation of 200,000 to 300,000. But, as Leslie Bruce, of the *Hollywood Reporter*, pointed out: 'A single tweet from the star can get a brand's name in front of nearly 9 million followers.' So it made sense for wedding products to pay to get a piece of the Kim Kardashian wedding action.

It was a marriage not so much made as minted. And like a coin, it was soon spent. After 72 days, Kardashian filed for a divorce. Humphries sought an annulment instead, reportedly claiming that the marriage was a fraud and strictly a TV event (an annulment declares a marriage never had a legal existence). Humphries' lawyer was quoted by the *Hollywood Reporter* as saying that the wedding 'was basically a contrivance for the benefit of her [Kardashian's] show and to make money' (August 19, 2012).

Kim and singer Kanye West had been long-term friends who got together after Kim's marriage broke down. Kanye rented out the AT&T baseball stadium in San Francisco to propose in 2013, turning what could have been a tender, private moment into something like the Super Bowl halftime show. He and Kardashian were known collectively as Kimye or K-squared. As Kardashian had taken the unauthorized leaking of a sex tape and turned it into a positive, West had, in 2009, snatched the mic from Taylor Swift at the annual MTV Video Music Awards and proclaimed Beyoncé's video for *Single Ladies (Put a Ring on it)* one of the best videos of all time. Before that, he declared on live television that then-president George Bush didn't care about black people, when commenting on the effects of Hurricane Katrina in 2005. Barack Obama famously described West as a jackass.

Lindsay Lohan was in the front row of West's inaugural 2011 runway show at Lycée Henri IV in Paris, where he unveiled a new line of clothes he'd designed and called Dw. The collection included, among other items, a fur backpack and a pair of $5,800 stiletto heels. West had already brokered a lucrative deal with Nike to design a line of footwear called Air Yeezy and was collaborating with Louis Vuitton on a range, though he later moved to adidas to produce Yeezy; the sportswear firm, in 2018, came under pressure to drop him after West's ill-chosen remarks on slavery were widely reported.

The combination of a gaffe-prone musician-cum-aspirant designer and a woman who had seemingly learned her trade – however unclassifiable – from Paris Hilton, prompted considerable curiosity. As the *USA Today* People Team put it: 'When Kardashian and West get together, the question shouldn't be "When is the wedding?" The question is: "What are they selling?"' (April 16, 2012). In this instance, the official answer was clothes, but, as ever, there was something else on sale.

'For me, a celebrity is somebody who is top of their game, a top film star, in music, whatever. I hate the word "celebrity".' When Elton John criticized breakout stars of reality TV shows for not 'earning' their stardom he was merely echoing a wider criticism of these new types of celebrity that others had made before and, no doubt, had been made throughout time. How might singers from the 1920s, who performed every night, have thought about artists who earned money from those big wax disks called records that that became popular in the 1940s. Nineteenth-century stage actors who worked every night must have sneered at screen actors who needed to play their role only once in front of a camera once silent film took off in the 1920s. You could probably find a time when entertainers of any kind were regarded contemptuously by those who earned their living in factories, or on farms. Performers in any period have a tendency to depreciate young tyros by comparing their achievements with their own and those of their contemporaries. (Sir Elton's comments are recorded by Natasha Sporn in her 2018 article for the Evening Standard.)"

What such a critique ignores is that audiences dictate taste. The Beatles were lambasted by some in the 1960s, just as hip-hop artists were in the 1980s. Talent, like beauty, is in the eye of beholder: it's the response that shapes *Please Please Me* (The Beatles, 1963) or *Rebel Without a Pause* (Public Enemy, 1987) into classics or cacophonies – and, ultimately, whether or not they earn fortunes for their makers. What is 'earn' anyway? Receiving a reward in exchange for labor or services? It doesn't matter what the activity, or, for that matter, the reward is, just as long as it's deservedly gained. Appearing on a TV show that draws viewers and involves them in a way they find agreeable is clearly not everyone's idea of an honestly earned living. But, like it or not, it actually is exactly that.

At some point, probably in 2005 or 2006, Kim Kardashian must have reflected on her friend Paris Hilton and wondered why someone who kept getting annihilated by critics every time she ventured into traditional entertainments, like acting or singing, was rising to vertiginous heights. It wasn't because she tried hard to please critics. She knew that audiences probably enjoyed witnessing her annihilation; and it was they, not the critics, who stumped up the money to pay for her products or to see her posing as a DJ or just sipping Cristal Brut at a nightclub. Kardashian must have noticed how Hilton's behavior unfailingly ensured favorable responses. As she oscillated ever more wildly between comedy and tragedy, consumers reacted. Part of the reaction was to spend money.

Years later in 2017, the British retail chain Superdrug delivered a 41 per cent year-on-year rise in profits after sales were pushed by a banana powder praised by Kardashian (it's a yellow toned setting powder that gives the face a sheen — like Kardashian's. 'Anyone can get their grid game on a par with Kim K.' the ad copy promised). By this time, the word influencer had entered the popular vocabulary. And Kardashian had the answer to her question.

When twitter launched in 2006, few people could have known how public fascination with celebrities would have turned this social networking site into a global marketing force. Facebook had been running for a couple of years and YouTube had disclosed the potential of user-generated content; in other words, inviting internet enthusiasts to upload and share videos or any other kind of data. Facebook-owned Instagram, the photo-sharing application didn't start till 2010, though its growth was formidable (by 2017 it had 700 million active users). For someone like Kardashian with no obvious skills but a very obvious audience, social networking was an almost natural fit. She joined twitter in March 2009, her exploits (sex tape, reality show, nude poses) already established.

The monetizing possibilities of social media were not immediately apparent, though some keen entrepreneurs sensed the potential. Chiara Ferragni, for example, started up a fashion blog, 'The Blonde Salad,' in 2009 then went on to launch her own line of shoes and collaborate with myriad brands, including Gucci and Guess. Susanna Lau launched Style Bubble in 2006, while working a day job in digital advertising; this was a year before people even had iPhones, which allowed them to browse the net on the move. In 2010, Danielle Bernstein launched her 'We Wore What' fashion blog. These were a kind of first generation of influencers in fashion, but there were others who advised on pets, parenting, travel, business, gaming, technology, health and fitness – practically every sphere of relevance.

The advertising wasn't overt: vloggers and bloggers just shared opinions and passed on hints, though, of course, a mention of branded products was advertising by another name. A mention carried potency because it reached an engaged, interested and motivated audience. Official advertising shifted markedly from about 2012: by 2017, ad agencies were spending more online than in traditional media. There is a school of thought that suggests advertising is most effective when it doesn't attract our conscious attention. We're most susceptible to influences when we're not aware that someone or something is even trying to influence us.

It's not known whether the Kardashian family members were adherents of this school (its earliest proponent was Walter Dill Scott, 1869-1955, whose book *The Psychology of Advertising* was first published in 1908), but they probably wouldn't have opposed it. Even if they did, they couldn't argue with the money ad agencies offered them to commend, approve, allude to, hint at, speak favorably of or just name a product. Kim could reach 9.4 million Instagram followers with one tap of her manicured index finger. Cost-benefit calculations led advertisers to believe that paying Kim up to $500,000 a time was decent value. Sisters Kendall and Kylie Jenner boasted 76.4 million and 89.1 million followers each (at the time of writing) and could only command $400,000 per post. Khloé, who had over 64 million followers, and Kourtney, with 54.3 million, could command $250,000 a time. Sir Elton, and established stars like him, might not have viewed this as 'earned' but for a man worth $500 million and who received $6.5 million (£5m) to appear in a TV ad for British retailer John Lewis in 2018, it seems to me to be unecessarily critical.

Writing in 1991 before the rise of digital media, the cultural historian Christopher Lasch argued that one of the main effects of the media was to 'to maintain the apparatus of addiction.' He didn't mean addiction to alcohol, tobacco or drugs, although Lasch reasoned that commodities 'alleviate boredom and satisfy the socially stimulated desire for novelty and excitement.' So maybe commodities *are* drugs. And maybe the 'logic of consumerism,' as Lasch called it in the 1990s, still dictates the way we and the media that surrounds and affects us operates. Facebook and the others had authenticity when they launched: they were a revolutionary form of connecting people's lives and shifting the manner in which social interaction was done. But they were all obliged to change in order to survive. In 2015, Mike Proulx, of the magazine *AdAge*, wrote an article with the headline THERE IS NO MORE SOCIAL MEDIA — JUST ADVERTISING. He was exaggerating, but only slightly.

Much as everyone loves sharing thoughts, experiences, images, videos, pieces of texts and any other kind of meme that can be copied and spread instantly, there is another side to social media: it's trying to sell us stuff. Influencer marketing might once have been an epiphenomenon, that is, a secondary effect or by-product of social media. But it's now an integral part of any social platform's vitality. Every sapient reader will know this. Every sapient reader will also have bought something online.

CHAPTER 6

SELFLESS SELVES

'When wealth occupies a higher position than wisdom, when notoriety is admired more than dignity, when success is more important than self-respect, the culture itself overvalues 'image' and must be regarded as narcissistic.' The passage is from Alexander Lowen's book *Narcissism: Denial of the True Self*, which was published in 1983. Lowen was a student of the Austrian psychotherapist Wilhelm Reich (1897-1957), author of the 1927 monograph *The Function of the Orgasm*. Lowen thought the three main features of the narcissistic society were: wealth, notoriety and success. And image. OK, four features. And its casualties were wisdom, dignity and self-respect. And image.

Before he became the Terminator and long before he was elected Governor of California, Arnold Schwarzenegger was Adonis. In Greek mythology, Adonis was the beautiful youth with a fabulous body, adored by goddesses Aphrodite and Persephone and a good many mortal females. In the 1970s, Arnold had his own legion of admirers. One of them, a woman, stripped naked in front of him and asked, 'Can you train this body for me?' Another offered to anoint his body with chocolate syrup then lick it clean. And the demand for his boudoir services was ceaseless. Attention like this was bound to make a man a little conceited. So, in 1976, when he agreed to have nude photographs taken for a spread in *Cosmopolitan*, he probably wasn't thinking straight. Imagine all those women going delirious at the sight of his pecs. He initially prevented the publication, though relented a year later and pictures of him lubed and in the buff were published in 1977.

Schwarzenegger thought of himself as a 'male Raquel Welch'. Welch was widely regarded as one of the most beguilingly desirable women in the world in the 1970s. This must have been an exhilarating way to think of himself. Although in 2003, five days before the election for the Governorship of California, in which Schwarzenegger was running, six women came forward to make accusations of sexual harassment, over a period from 1975 to the early 2000s. Schwarzenegger prevailed in that election and became the state's Governor. Denying some of the accusations specifically, he also acknowledged that he had sometimes "behaved badly" on film sets and later that he had "learned my lesson" and that he had taken anti-harassment classes".

His looks were, of course, his fortune; he seemed to feature caveman-like in every action movie of the 1980s and his stock phrases, like 'I'll be back' and 'Hasta la vista, baby' are still part of our lexicon. Vanity in others usually meets with scorn and derision, though in Schwarzenegger's case, it became part of the iconic hardware. A Schwarzenegger without the bluster and swollen head wouldn't really be Arnie; he'd be just another egotistical actor with big biceps and good teeth, and they were ten a penny in Hollywood.

The disquieting quality that Schwarzenegger had and no one else dared to criticize was braggadocio. Somehow he could charm and alienate people simultaneously. If anyone else behaved so arrogantly, people would have thought, 'What a big-headed poseur!' Instead they smiled, 'It's Arnie. He's different.' And so he became a standard-bearer, leading the way for a generation to deliver a new message: loving yourself is nothing to be embarrassed about; it's a wonderful thing; embrace it. In 1977, George Benson's hit *The Greatest Love of All* captured the mood: 'Learning to love yourself/It is the greatest love of all' (later covered by Whitney Houston without 'The' in the title).

William E. Wycislo, a professor of classics, believes: 'The nature of tyrannies, whether of the first or the twentieth century, is such that it necessarily establishes a political milieu in which the narcissist can assume a respected public role, enforce public policy, and receive reinforcement for the very traits Freud and his disciples would consider symptoms of pathology.' It's a matter of judgement whether the USA in the 2000s had a government cruel and oppressive enough to be called tyrannical, but what is more certain is that there was a milieu in which a narcissist could be respected and elected and still qualify as pathological in the early 21st century than if they had lived in the late nineteenth or early twentieth centuries. In fact, it's possible that a whole generation would be diagnosed by Sigmund Freud (1856-1939) as certifiable.

Narcissism is one of those words we use, usually as part of a criticism, but without considering exactly what it means. Its source is Narcissus. So here goes our second visit to Greek mythology in this chapter: Narcissus was a man of great beauty (another one) on whom the nymph Echo was fixated. She wasn't alone; women and men alike lusted after Narcissus, but he was more interested in hunting deer. Exhausted from running during one hunt, Narcissus rested near a river and bent over to take a drink. On seeing his own reflection, he was smitten. Of course, every time he tried to kiss the image, it disappeared, leaving him tormented and, eventually, he wasted away from lack of food and water. There are several variations on the myth, but the central parable is of the handsome man who was so obsessed with his own reflection that he destroyed himself. Is the moral clear enough? Self-love is not a good thing.

Like other myths, this one came with a warning. Narcissus was cursed not by his good looks but by his preoccupation with himself; he became self-absorbed to the point where he mistook his own image as an independent being. Freud had a field day with the myth and diagnosed a condition that successive waves of psychologists and psychiatrists have elaborated into narcissistic personality disorder, which basically describes a condition of excessive admiration of or interest in oneself, in particular one's physical appearance, and an extreme selfishness, with a grandiose conception of one's own talents and a longing for approval. According to an eleven-strong team of psychologists led by Frederick S. Stinson, 7.7 per cent of men and 4.8 per cent of women in the USA have narcissistic personality disorder at some point in their lives.

The disorder is, as the name suggests, an unhealthy condition, though, as Pat MacDonald, of the UK Council for Psychotherapy, points out, there is a healthy narcissism, which 'involves a steady sense of one's worth, based on genuine achievement, the capacity to recover from disappointment or failure and the ability to find comfort and support in relationships.' MacDonald believes: 'We are all on a continuum between healthy and unhealthy narcissism.' Trapped, we assume, like Narcissus, in torments that are part enabling, part subjugating.

The spirit and temperament of the times can shift whole populations along the continuum, and what MacDonald calls the 'age of entitlement' has pushed us all away from the healthy extremity. While she doesn't actually define this age of entitlement, MacDonald is undoubtedly thinking of the ethos that inspires us to think that we deserve privileges and treatment that were not available to previous generations; we feel we have a right to prioritize our own well-being and take the opportunity to realize whatever potential we suspect we have.

MacDonald thinks there are obvious casualties: 'There is ample evidence that common mental health disorders, such as anxiety, depression, panic attacks, as well as an inability to experience pleasure have all significantly increased. We have seen a sharp rise in drug taking, anti-social behavior, binge drinking and shallow sexuality.'

I'm not quite so Aristotelian in my acceptance of empirical evidence. For instance, the rise in rates of depression and other mental illnesses is more likely a sign of our diagnostic tendencies that are, in turn, affected by the availability of pharmaceuticals to treat conditions. These have made possible therapies for previously unnamed conditions. Indulging excessively in alcohol or drugs or, for that matter, shallow sex (whatever that is) are hardly new recreations. Statistics are not necessarily reliable guides to social change; how we compile, understand and react to them are. All the same, MacDonald seems to have her finger on the social pulse even if her stress on the psychotherapeutic means she's unable to analyze the deeper changes that affect the way we all think.

Question: Would Schwarzenegger have become a celebrity if he hadn't moved from his native Austria to the USA at the age of 21, in 1968? Or would he have been a noted body-builder with a belief that he was God's gift? Answers not required. Remember: context is everything.

Thorstein Veblen (1857–1929) thought he was being sarcastic about the inelegant exhibitionism he saw all around him in 1899 when he first wrote about what he called *conspicu-ous consumption*. The American economist noticed how peo-ple were beginning to attach unwarranted importance to things; things being the products or commodities that were being manufactured, then bought, sold and eventually dis-carded as unwanted waste. The traditional functional approach to shopping was simple: when consumers needed stuff, they bought it; when they didn't, they didn't buy it. But Veblen noticed how affluent people were buying all sorts of things to display how well-off they were. It was a way of flaunting their affluence.

Interest in consumer items withered with familiarity: as people grew tired of their possessions, they lost interest. So what did they do? Exactly. They bought new replacements. The title of Veblen's book was The Theory of the Leisure Class. The new class wasn't a bit embarrassed about their money; they felt they deserved it through hard work and some ingenuity. The stuff they bought still had utility, of course; just not as much as its price suggested. A shirt, for example, is still a form of protective clothing, even if is a bar-oque print Gucci costing $700 (we'll return to one such shirt later). But that same shirt could do much more than just protect.

Veblen probably sneered at the exhibitionism of the newly emerging class and its tendency to buy just to demonstrate status, prestige and money. They were showing off (and were likely to be wearing Worth rather than Gucci, this being a Parisian haute couture house, 1858–1954). Whether he liked what he saw or not, Veblen was divining the future: con-spicuous consumption became one of the phrases of the cen-tury. Consumers became aspirational, constantly seeking to upgrade their possessions as a way of showing others what progress they were making – progress, that is, as they wanted others to see it.

The tendency became more pronounced in the years after the First World War (1914–1918) when the large manufacturers faced over-production. If shoppers bought strictly according to need, they simply wouldn't spend enough to keep the mass-production industries in profit. Somehow, they had to be encouraged to see shoes, food, homes or other products as more than practical solutions to practical problems.

Harry Selfridge visualized a solution of sorts. He was born in America in 1858, but travelled to London and, in 1909, opened a store that bore his name. It had about 100 departments plus restaurants, roof gardens and reading rooms. A visit to Selfridge's was an experience rather than a transaction. In New York, Macy & Co had moved toward a similar type of establishment, which had also been employed in Paris by Le Bon Marché, though it wasn't until 1924 when Macy's doubled its size that it began its growth to be America's biggest department store. In one sense, department stores catered to the emerging demand for consumer products though, in another, they were parts of a new rhythm of life: a strong, regular, repeated pattern of behavior in which people didn't just shop, but enjoyed the experience of shopping.

The Great Depression (1929–1939) interrupted this, though economic measures introduced by President Franklin D. Roosevelt in 1933 restored confidence and effectively kick-started the economy. In 1938, the sociologist Robert K. Merton published the results of his influential study of 'a society, which places a high premium on economic affluence and ascent for all its members,' i.e., America. Merton's focus was 'the central motivating impulse in American life – pursuit of the American dream,' wrote Robert C. Hauhart in his 2015 article on 'American Sociology's Investigations of the American Dream.'

By the late 1930s, when Merton was writing, the success embodied in the Dream had been reduced to one dimension:

money. Merton (1910–2003) was at pains to expose the
workings of a 'system of cultural values [that] extols, above
all else, certain common symbols of success … while its
social structure rigorously restricts or completely eliminates
access to approved modes of acquiring these symbols.' In
other words, as Hauhart put it, 'most individuals will not
become monetarily successful.' This didn't stop them craving.

Hollywood stars were success incarnate: they not only
lived the kind of life to which all Americans, to some degree,
aspired, but they embodied an ideal – they could buy anything they wanted. Merton was fascinated by how much
ordinary people wanted to pursue the same path to material
fulfilment and how some discovered shortcuts. By this, he
meant they turned to crime. Hollywood played a role in
maintaining the success ethic and, while Merton wasn't especially interested in the film industry, he offered a way of
understanding how material success filtered all the way
through society and affected everyone. Products that were, in
earlier periods, ordinary inanimate objects, carried intoxicat-
ing promises: they could express the way we thought about
ourselves and how we wanted others to think about us.

What changed us from functional consumers to aspirational status-seekers? The answer was hardly a secret to anyone who read newspapers, listened to the radio, went to the
cinema, or after the 1950s, watched television. Advertising
was everywhere; citizens just couldn't escape the craft of *The
Hidden Persuaders*. This was the title of Vance Packard's
1957 book, which was part-analysis, part-warning and part-
tribute to an industry that had successfully turned practically
everyone into endlessly dissatisfied consumers, who wanted
to buy merchandise. The tribute part was unintentional:
Packard was critical of the mind-bending psychoanalytical
techniques advertisers used to manipulate our longings without our knowledge. But the book presented a chilling

masterclass in how ad agencies had drawn on Freud and several of his acolytes to create a kind of legitimate, benevolent coercion.

This entailed engaging not with the more rational or logical aspects of our character – *Homo economicus*, as economists call this model – but the less apparent, reasonless aspects. Here are two minor examples. Betty Crocker cake mix had made its product too convenient; in other words, women (and remember the era) simply had to stir with water, place in the oven and turn on the heat. Sales suffered until female focus groups yielded a prescription: ask the cook to do something, like add an egg and a splash of milk, and they became active in the gastronomy. It worked and sales picked up.

The Freudian input to what became known as motivational research was more pronounced in a campaign to encourage women to smoke cigarettes. One of those Freud acolytes I mentioned earlier was Ernest Dichter (1907–1991), who coaxed the participation of women in the pursuit before it was known that inhaling tobacco smoke was self-destructive. Dichter claimed women smoked more when ads showed cigarettes in the hands of other women so advertisers were advised to feature pictures of women, particularly glamorous women, in advertisements. Dichter theorized that women experienced penis envy, so holding a phallic appurtenance between their fingers satisfied their crypto-sexual desires. Dichter also advised the toy manufacturer Mattel to increase the size of the Barbie doll's breasts.

These were instances of what Packard called an attempt 'to channel our unthinking habits, our purchasing decisions, and our thought processes by the use of insights gleaned from psychiatry.' The postwar period was a time of relative affluence; women were the choice demographic, but teens and, later, pre-teens were slyly courted as potential buyers. Behind the psychoanalytical theory, the basic mechanism that kept consumer society ticking involved stimulating discontents or desires, then holding out a promise to satisfy them with buy-able products. The approach was not unlike therapy, by which I mean a treatment intended to relieve or heal a dis-order. The implication of this was that buying products had a good effect on the body and mind and contributed to a sense of well-being. The central idea is obvious enough today: we all want to approach or reach the state of being comfortable, healthy and happy. At least, this is my understanding of well-being. Everybody wants it. This is linked via a connective tis-sue of advertising, marketing and global corporations to our interest in ourselves. I repeat: this is obvious enough today. But it wasn't always so. Personal satisfactions, or 'growth,' weren't always individuals' priorities. So, what happened?

American forces began leaving Vietnam in 1973, the war coming to a conclusion two years later. Following the USA's military engagement in 1964, there had been a growing pro-test, complemented by the civil rights movement, mostly among young people. The 'peace and love' ethos of hippies was developed in response to the war. Civil rights marches and sit-ins had been dealt with brutally by the police and state troopers. The rise of television in the 1950s meant that most people could stare at their screens in disbelief as the American state brought its force to bear, primarily on black people. Perhaps in the late 1960s, no one seriously thought that the same force would be directed at whites. After all, blacks had been slaves up to a hundred years before (the Emancipation Proclamation was made in 1862) and their lives had been restricted by segregation ever since. Seeing them struck down, beaten mercilessly and sometimes killed by law enforcement officers and the military was horrifying, but expected. White protestors were something else.

The anti-Vietnam movement wasn't exactly good vs evil: America was divided and, while sentiment against the war was rising in proportion to lives lost (officially, there were 58,220 American military deaths during the war), public opinion was by no means behind campaigners. On May 4 1970, at Kent State University, 15 miles from Akron, members of the Ohio National Guard opened fire on unarmed demonstrators protesting the illegal bombing of Cambodia by US forces a few days before. About 67 rounds were fired, killing four students and wounding nine. The incident transfigured the dialogue, national and international, on Vietnam. But it also helped shape a new vision of social change. Young people were free to challenge and confront America's power bloc all they wished – but not with impunity. Objecting to the war was allowable in the land of the free; but expressing disapproval involved running a dangerous gauntlet. Being white was no protection.

The Kent State killings made denial impossible; no one could refuse to recognize that the peace and love embraced by young people couldn't be achieved painlessly, if at all. Civil rights was a shining example of how change could be achieved through collective efforts. From December 1, 1955, when Rosa Parks refused to give up her seat on a Montgomery City bus, till July 2, 1964, when the landmark Civil Rights Act was passed, African Americans had worked in unison, their persistent defiance demonstrating how collective action could be effective, if often agonizing. The petrifying glimpse of state force at Kent State plunged American youth into anomie, their usual social and ethical standards liquefied, their image of a new society gone. In its place, a new image emerged; one that involved a lot less trauma and tribulation.

'People today hunger not for personal salvation,' observed Christopher Lasch in the 1970s, 'but for the feeling, the momentary illusion, of personal well-being, health, and psychic security.' A despair of changing society had, according to Lasch, inclined protesting citizens away from politics and collective action and toward 'expanded consciousness, health, and personal growth.' He used this phrase in a *New York Review of Books* article, in which he focused on the 'erosion of the concern for posterity,' by which he meant that people lived for themselves in the present and had no interest in future (or for that matter past) generations. The narcissistic personalities we referred to earlier set off a kind of contagion in the 1970s. People turned inwards, replacing thoughts of changing society with reflections on how to change themselves as individuals.

Unlike psychologists, who regarded – and still regard – narcissism as a type of personality condition, or disorder, Lasch saw a pervasive change in the very structure of psychic life. And that change was affected by 'quite specific changes in our society and culture,' which included consumption and the rise of a therapeutic sensibility – we became responsive to ideas about how to enhance our well-being, in other words. Consumerism was already the engine of the American economy. Lasch wrote that the same capitalism that had licensed advertisers and their motivational experts to get inside our heads and discover how best to make us spend money had given rise to *The Culture of Narcissism*, as he called it in the title of his book.

As the retreat from mass protest and collective resistance gathered pace, so the concept of personal transformation took hold and the apparatus of supply-and-demand was ready. What mattered in life was not structural social change, but self-improvement. People wanted to get in touch 'with their own feelings,' eat healthy food, take regular exercise, immerse themselves in Zen, yoga or other transcendental enlightenments of the East. Harmless in themselves, mused

Lasch, these pursuits signalled a shift from the political and social upheavals of the 1960s (race riots, as well as civil rights, college disruptions, and antiwar protests). Instead people oriented toward living for the moment – and for themselves. One major result of this was that they became atomized: separated like the droplets of a fine spray of liquid.

'The contemporary climate is therapeutic.' Lasch's point wasn't that everyone rushed into therapy as patients, but they were leaning over the water, staring as lovestruck as Narcissus, and wondering how they could enhance themselves, yet with few plans beyond their immediate needs and no plans at all to change the world. In a sense, people 'liberated' themselves from political responsibilities and commitments to great causes and turned inwards, seeking personal solutions to private concerns, which may have been physical, though they were equally likely to be spiritual and more than likely to be both.

Think about yourself today: you're encouraged to exercise regularly, eat healthily, seek counsel at the first suspicion of mental health 'issues' (as what used to be known as problems have been rephrased), and never bottle up anything. As I write, my email inbox shows an alert for a one-day university event bearing the title 'Work-Life Balance, Mental Health and Wellbeing.' So many aspects of culture today are powered by energy sourced from the 1970s. 'Today's youth, the Generation Me, is deemed materialistic, entitled, and narcissistic,' wrote Dutch communications professors Suzanna Johanna Opree and Rinaldo Kühne in 2016. So where did materialism and entitlement come from?

Materialism, the tendency to consider material possessions and physical comfort life's priorities, is easier to explain. Lasch quoted Jerry Rubin, a onetime Yippie (a politically active hippie) who retreated from his activism and explored 'est, gestalt therapy, bioenergetics, rolfing, massage, jogging, health foods, tai chi, Esalen, hypnotism, modern dance, meditation, Silva Mind Control, Arica, acupuncture, sex therapy, Reichian therapy, and More House.' (I won't explain them all, but 'est' was Erhard Seminar Training, a cultish consciousness awakening, Esalen was a retreat in southern California, Silva Mind Control, now just Silva, is a meditation method, Reichian therapy is a way of releasing suppressed anger and frustration, based on the methods of the previously mentioned Wilhelm Reich. I'll leave the reader to Google the others.) Personal growth wasn't the only unifying feature of these endeavours. As Lasch noted: 'the new therapies are usually expensive.' Individual self-realization and the restoration of wholeness, like many other desirable features in life, didn't come cheap. Subtle enticements to self-improve were accompanied by less subtle demands for money.

Transgressive as they seemed, the inner-explorers of the new culture in the 1970s were still consumers. And it didn't take long for an industry to catch up. Perhaps the most spectacularly successful initiative of the narcissism industry was Jane Fonda's 90-minute video, originally titled *Workout, starring Jane Fonda* and later better known as *Jane Fonda's Workout*. The video was released a year after Fonda's *Workout Book*, which had been published in 1981 – the year in which MTV was launched. While aerobics classes were filling up across the world, not everyone wanted to squeeze into clingy gear and cavort energetically in the company of others. Fonda's video instructed beginners on how to get in shape without fear of embarrassment and without the expense of joining a gym. All you needed was a room and a VCR (videocassette recorders were state-of-the-art technology in early 1980s).

Over the next several years, Fonda's original video sold 17 million copies and spawned 23 specialist tapes (exercise for pregnant women, working out with weights and so on). As Jane Fonda the actor famed for *Klute* (1971) and *9 to 5* (1980) faded from view, Fonda the workout guru shone like a beacon, guiding a generation toward regular exercise and all-round well-being. She was almost 45 when the video was released. It's still available on DVD for about ten dollars.

Also released in the early 1980s, though without the acclaim or the longevity of Fonda's video was *Shape Up With Arnold Schwarzenegger* (1982). Fonda was a long-established movie star, while Schwarzenegger was still two years away from his breakthrough *Terminator* role. He'd appeared as himself in a popular feature-length documentary *Pumping Iron* and had starring parts as *Conan the Barbarian*, but had yet to register on the A-list. In the early 1980s, he was but one of literally hundreds of others who produced their own exercise guides, all keyed to a population that no longer considered perfecting their minds and bodies an indulgence of the 1970s – and, perhaps more importantly, was prepared to pay for perfection. Or at least for perfectibility.

Today, caring for ourselves, body and mind isn't remotely unusual. Doesn't everyone? Haven't we always? The answers are yes and no. It's almost unthinkable that we don't pay close attention to and spend money on ourselves; this isn't extravagance. Facial treatments, supplements, spas, exercise equipment: we pay for well-being. But, we didn't start doing this shamelessly until the 1970s, and, in the 1980s, this shifted up a gear.

Designer labels were unheard of till around 1980. The Paul Schrader film *American Gigolo* (1980) effectively introduced the world to Giorgio Armani and, from there, dressing turned into a sort of one-upmanship. By the end of the decade, the term conspicuous consumption, as Veblen called it at the end of the nineteenth century, was still accurate, but only in the way the first production Model T Ford is accurately called a car. It doesn't look much like the convertible 450SL Mercedes Benz coupé Richard Gere drove in the Schrader movie.

The accoutrements of narcissism, the cultural phenomenon, were things: personal belongings, equipment, clothes, cars, jewelry, anything that expressed who people were, or at least who they wanted others to think they were. All things were replaceable, or 'upgradable.' They would begin to obsolesce almost as soon as they were purchased, anyway. Experiencing well-being and enjoying a satisfying feeling of contentment (or security, happiness, or whatever someone sought) wasn't enough in the 1980s. People felt the need to represent themselves, their beauty, wealth or possession of what some writers call cultural capital, the cluster of symbolic assets like taste, posture, speech, mannerisms and proficiencies that distinguish us from some and align us with others.

At the risk of testing the reader's patience, I repeat: we take this for granted today. Surely, most people are self-aware enough to realize that every day, they are involved in a presentation – a presentation of self, as the sociologist Erving Goffman called it. Goffman's imagining of social interaction as a form of theater with people striving to manage a particular kind of impression of themselves was a hugely original and path-breaking approach to social life when it was first published in 1956. Thirty years later it was obvious. By then, the costumes and props Goffman wrote about had become known as *signifiers*, that is, the physical expression of meanings or ideas (the meaning itself was called the *signified*).

Clothes and accessories were also used in a self-conscious way as a form of ambulant advertising; people became advertisements. Look around you and try to identify as many brands worn or carried by other people. You'll see the Nike swoosh on somebody's shoes or tee-shirt, someone slurping from a cup, which you'll know from the mermaid symbol is Starbucks, possibly listening to music through earbuds bearing the lowercase "b" that tells us they're Beats. Advertising in Packard's day and for the next quarter century after his book, was a case of *them* and *us*: they advertised wares and we were supposed to be persuaded to buy them. In the changed scheme of things, narcissistic consumers became moving ads. Again, this seems glaringly obvious today. But look at images of athletes, entertainers and ordinary citizens in the 1970s or before and you won't see a label, insignia, logo or any giveaway at all. Well, not unless you look hard, in which case you can see the Lacoste crocodile motif on some tennis players' shirts. Or Keith Richards' distinctive guitar, a Fender Telecaster.

Today, no one criticizes advertising's surreptitious influence or its stealthy creep into all facets of our lives. We don't seem to mind this. Objections usually center on some offensive aspect of advertising. Pepsi pulled a campaign featuring Kendall Jenner in 2017. Consumers complained that it trivialized demonstrations aimed at tackling social causes. Jenner was shown stepping away from a modeling shoot to join a crowd of young, diverse protesters before offering a can of Pepsi to a cop.

Heineken, in 2018, removed a commercial that showed a bartender sliding a bottle of its light beer past a number of black people before it reached a light-skinned female. Some interpreted this as racist. You'll see the red, white and blue Pepsi globe insignia on caps, cups, phone stands, towels and many more items. The star symbol of Heineken appears on glasses, luggage, iPhone cases, hoodies and merchandise associated with Formula 1 and UEFA Champions League soccer, which they co-sponsor. In other words, we do the advertising just by using the products.

———————————

When Lasch wrote of a culture of narcissism, he didn't imply that a whole generation of people had narcissistic personality disorder — if indeed there is such a thing; psychiatrists are prolific diagnosticians of pathological conditions. A culture describes the ideas, values, standards, attitudes and action of people, the codes they subscribe to and the norms, or typical patterns of behavior they usually try to follow. As a species, Homo sapiens have probably always been prone to self-consciousness and an inchoate vanity. But, if you accept Lasch's account of history, the 1970s was a game-changing decade. And, if you accept mine, so was the 2000s.

At the turn of the century there was no escape from everything that seemed to Lasch to be features of a new landscape. Gone, or at least fast disappearing, were the tenets of diligence, sobriety, sacrifice, frugality and discipline, all of which were associated with the Protestant ethic. Instead, there was a society of abundance, ruled by market forces, advertising and easy credit and 'encouraged by a consumerist mentality that promoted immediate gratification and living for the moment as the highest aims in life,' to use author Rochelle Gurstein's phrase. We welcomed the intervention of therapists into what were traditionally regarded as private affairs; privacy itself was radically reevaluated — as I'll explore in the next chapter.

The near-obsessive interest in the self was novel when Lasch was writing; in 2002, Christina Aguilera's *Beautiful*, with its reminder, 'I am beautiful in every single way,' was hailed as an empowering anthem, praised by LGBTQ+ and cis groups alike. Anyone who followed the song's message could interpret it somewhat differently as a paean to self-love. And not unlike the Right Said Fred send-up of 1991, *I'm Too Sexy* ("So sexy it hurts"). But the reception for the Aguilera ballad suggested that pride was no longer one of the seven deadly sins: a belief in one's worth had morphed into a good thing. In fact, honoring and taking care of oneself was nearly an obligation. People were inclined to feel guilty if they didn't attend to their well-being. Narcissism became, to use a word of the twenty-first century, *normalized*; put another way, it was such a customary or ordinary condition that we don't even notice it; it's just a natural state of affairs.

If we could lease one of those DeLoreans from the *Back to the Future* films and speed back to 1985, when the first of the movies was released, it would be interesting to gauge the reaction to what I imagine most of us would do within thirty seconds of landing: whip out a phone, stand in front of something that exudes 1980s-ness (a record shop with cassettes on sale; a car bearing a faded bumper sticker Reagan-Bush '84) and take a selfie. By the time onlookers realized what was going on, the moment would be over and the phone would be turned around to show the resulting picture. The response would be one of amazement or derision: *Wow!* or *What a jerk!* Or people might just crack up laughing at the sight of someone indulging in what they would have considered a photographic equivalent of self-abuse. This is 1985, remember. Twenty-five years later, no one was laughing.

Committing images of ourselves to posterity is not new. Rembrandt (1606–1669) painted over 90 pictures of himself. Frida Kahlo (1907–1954) is perhaps the most acclaimed female proponent; at least, before 2015. Marketing professors Richard Kedzior and Douglas E. Allen, in a scholarly article subtitled 'Understanding the Selfie Experience,' remind us: 'Self-portraiture as an artistic tradition dates back to the Renaissance period.' That's in the fourteenth to the sixteenth centuries. Photographs became possible as soon as the French physicist Louis Daguerre presented his invention in 1839, though, according to Kedzior and Allen, self-taken photos became more popular in the 1970s, and then surged with the

'the proliferation of digital cameras, which made producing selfies easy and cost-effective.' That would have been from the mid-1990s.

Digital cameras don't need film, of course. The Kodak DC-25 was the first camera to use CompactFlash cards, which enabled users to take photos and send them via a modem to computers, though the compact Casio QV-10, at about $1,000, was the most popular digital camera of the period. In 2002, Sanyo launched its SCP-5300, a clamshell style phone that incorporated a camera. This was one of those technological contraptions that, at first, prompt people to ask, 'Why would anyone want that?' and then make them reflect, 'How did we manage without it?' The same with television, microwaves and sundry other gadgets that are indispensable to modern life. A similar device had been available in Japan twelve months before, but didn't take off. But, by the end of 2003, 80 million camera phones had been sold worldwide.

The word selfie had been in use for a couple of years before the *Oxford English Dictionary* decided it should properly be included in its corpus in 2013. The editors claimed an astonishing 17,000 per cent increase in frequency of usage in the previous twelve months. Don't underestimate the power of a label in transforming what was once an odd enterprise into a respectable, social practice. Posing in front of one's own camera phone in public and sharing it would have looked the height of peacockery (which practically every dictionary defines as 'ostentatious display'). Well, it would have done before, say, 2012. After, it became as commonplace as air kissing.

I called the dictionary editors' claim of a 17,000 per cent increase astonishing, but this pales beside the growth of selfies since 2013. In 2015, 24 billion selfies were posted on Google's servers. Writing in 2016, David Cohen of *AdWeek* converted the 93 million selfies taken each day into the old-style film: they represented 2,583,333 rolls. One thousand selfies were posted to Instagram every 10 seconds, according to Cohen. Perhaps most surprising is that only 55 per cent of Millennials (broadly speaking, people born 1981–2001) had taken selfies and shared them via social media (I suspect this is an underestimate, probably caused by sampling error or research participants' flippancy).

Selfies are, for many people 'indicators of toxic self-centredness and self-obsession,' as Katrin Tiidenberg put it in her book *Selfies*. Totems of narcissism. When Kim Kardashian collected 300 self-portraits into a book, she called them 'a candid tribute to my fans.' For many, the very idea of curating a collection of selfies was the height of pomposity: it wasn't so much a tribute as an expression of disdain. This would miss the point. Kardashian was, by popular consent, the queen of the selfies, someone who had seized on the genre (I think I can legitimately call it that) and used it to show that she wasn't just a pretty face. And, even if she was just a pretty face, it was a face that would be replicated a limitless number of times and become the subject of inspections, reproductions and interrogations.

A face that also earned money: *Selfish*, the 352-page book, logged 125,000 in sales at between $10–20. Three years after the book's publication, Kardashian declared: 'I don't take selfies anymore, I don't really like them. It's not all about sitting there taking selfies, I just like to live there in real life.' Thus proving that, with resolve, people can overcome even the most ingrained, debilitating passions. At least that's how Janarthanan Balakrishnan and Mark D. Griffiths understand what they consider the obsessive talking of selfies, a condition they label 'selfitis.'

Kardashian was posting photos of herself online before people were using the word 'selfie'. She favored twitter, which launched in 2007 and then Instagram from 2010. The latter was the perfect vehicle, being a picture-sharing network. (It was acquired by Facebook in 2012.) Why was it perfect? Because Kardashian initially didn't have what Hilton did: inescapability. The media trailed Hilton everywhere, ensuring her image was ever-present everywhere."

In social media, Kardashian had a relatively new conduit: why would she need photographers and reporters shadowing her every movement when she could just take pictures of herself and post them online. Then the rapid, exponential multiplication known as going viral would make those images almost impossible to avoid – inescapable. The beauty of this process was that as social media grew in stature so traditional media began to mine it for stories. Kardashian was a story. By 2015, the year of her book's publication, she had 42 million Instagram followers. Taylor Swift had 45.5 million, but considering Kardashian didn't sing or play an instrument, it was no mean achievement, no doubt assisted by her relationship with a celebrity. Swift also had amorous relationships with celebrities: she was between Harry Styles and Calvin Harris at the time.

Speaking of Harry Styles: he was a known to be fond of Gucci. He was regularly seen wearing the Italian designer label's suits, loafers and shirts. One such shirt, a blazing red one, had a similar effect on his fans as would have had on a raging bull. In spring, 2017 The Naked Diet author Tess Ward innocently (we presume) posted a picture of herself wearing a shirt identical to one owned by Styles on Instagram. It was all the confirmation his admirers needed that she and Styles were an item. Ward must have conjectured how her life would have had an alternate history had she resisted the temptation to hit 'send' and instead, pushed 'delete.' Julia Llewellyn Smith, of The Australian sums up what happened after she posted: 'She became a 21st-century Yoko Ono, loathed by loyal Directioners [fans of Styles and his former bandmates from One Direction], who are notorious for making voodoo dolls and sending death threats to any woman with whom their idols socialize.' (Yoko Ono was John Lennon's partner from the mid-1960s to his death in 1980; many Beatles fans concluded she was responsible for the fragmentation of the band, sullying Paul McCartney and, generally, having a damaging effect on Lennon's music – this was before the internet.)

There was a sudden backlash against Ward, starting with a multiplication of 1★ ratings for her cookbook on Amazon. After this came a merciless trolling on Instagram and Ward implored her new followers to 'be kind.' It was a naïve imploration and motivated fans to greater efforts. Directioners, as loyal followers of the boyband (which announced an indefinite 'hiatus' in 2016) called themselves, were pitiless fans. No devotee welcomes love interest such as this. Instagram and other social media platforms offer unprecedented access to celebrities; never in history have audiences been able to engage in an almost intimate way with public figures. Fans can track their idols' day-to-day movements and perhaps even get a 'like' or a reply. There's a tradeoff though: fans feel a sense of entitlement. So when a pop star like Styles starts, or even appears to start, a relationship with someone, there is no chance of keeping it private: it becomes known immediately. That much is taken for granted. But, when the new partner flaunts online, she might as well be rubbing the fans' noses in it.

The experience of another One Direction member, Louis Tomlinson, should have served notice. In 2016, it became known that his partner Briana Jungwirth was pregnant with his child. Jungwirth might have been expecting congratulatory messages on her social media feeds. Instead she was treated to an unstoppable online invective that included death threats. This is the source of the entitlement I mentioned earlier in this chapter, when discussing the research of the Dutch professors Opree and Kühne and it's why I resist claiming that the emergence of social media and selfies is yet another extension of the narcissism we've been charting in this chapter.

'In space, no one can hear you scream.' At least according to the advertising for the 1979 Ridley Scott movie *Alien*. But, in cyberspace, everyone can hear you – at least potentially. They can also see you and read what you write. That's the beauty of the internet: no one censors or edits and everyone is free to share whatever he or she please, regardless of whether others take offence. Social media generally and selfies in particular made celebrities answerable to the very people who created and maintained them. Obviously, the traditional media were instrumental in elevating celebs to prominence, but audiences determined whether they stayed that way, or were consigned to oblivion.

In 2015 Caitlin Flanagan, of the *New York Times*, asked how people should understand Kim Kardashian and fashioned an answer from another question: 'As exemplar, as someone with much to teach us about mastering our own selfish lives?' Yes, Kardashian is an exemplar of aspiration and even a paradigm of imperfect ordinariness – something which I'll come to in the next chapter. But mastering our own selfish lives? If people are as selfish as Flanagan supposes, why do we share so much? We still have individualistic feelings and susceptibilities, taking care of ourselves, seeking therapeutic interventions whenever available and ceding responsibilities for our own faults to others, or anonymous institutions. We also share, arguably more than at any time in history. Some say we *over*-share.

Our selfish selves are more benevolent than Flanagan supposes. Millennials and the poor, in particular are charitable narcissists. The cohort born following Generation X give more generously, particularly at Christmas, than previous generations, though they're more careful in checking out the charities to which they donate. In the UK, the annual income of charities is more than the nation's total defence budget. About 30 per cent of Americans living below the poverty level gave to charity, according to a 2016 study by Patricia Snell Herzog and Heather E. Price. A sceptic might respond that this is merely narcissism mutating and that giving money away or spending it on others makes people feel happier than spending it on themselves and, even more counterintuitively, giving to others can actually make us healthier. Michael Sanders and Francesca Tamma of the *Guardian*'s behavioral insights team confirm this in their 'The Science Behind Why People Give Money to Charity.'

In 2017, Susan Shelley, of the *Los Angeles Daily News* wrote of 'The Explosive Growth of Panhandling.' While there's no reliable figures to suggest whether or not panhandling, or more passive forms of begging have increased in recent years, prosecutions either for aggressive acts or just importuning in parts where there are local ordinances against it tell us it still goes on. And it goes on, logically enough, because there are people who give out of the goodness of their heart; motivated by kindness and generosity rather than the expectation of any personal gain (apart from moral purification, maybe), people simply give.

The excessive and tasteless extravagance we associate with celebrities might, at another time, in another place, elicit feelings of resentment or dislike. Yet somehow, celebrities manage to keep in favor, possibly because they cleanse themselves metaphorically when they perform dutifully for charities, like UNICEF, Oxfam, the Red Cross. Organizations like these undoubtedly benefit from having the services of Taylor Swift, Miley Cyrus, Sean Combs and other entertainers who have either made cash contributions – Mel Gibson donated $10 million to children's hospitals – or devoted time to humanitarian projects. Angelina Jolie was a United Nations Special Envoy and toured areas of conflict, for example in northern Iraq. Cynics try to dismiss their contributions as meretricious and sensationalist, designed only to grab headlines. I don't resent the excesses and I don't dismiss the contributions.

Narcissism, as we understand it today, has not turned people into insular, inconsiderate, unsympathetic, mean-spirited tightwads. It probably hasn't turned everyone into neighbourly, considerate, sympathetic, thoughtful, munificent philanthropists, either. But, there's nothing inconsistent about being all these and still maintaining a close watch on one's appearance, one's health and one's all-round state of well-being. In the 1970s, the accent on the self seemed excessive and tasteless after decades of turmoil and rebellion. In subsequent years, new generations made a virtue out of what seemed and probably was once a vice.

Question: In 2009, the Governor of California Arnold Schwarzenegger signed a new bill into law Sunday that penalized paparazzi for taking photos that violated a celebrity's right to privacy. Eleven years before, Schwarzenegger, then a movie star, had his car swarmed by paparazzi while he was picking up his child from school; it was inconvenient but essential for celebrities to have paps in close pursuit. If he had the power to make changes in the law in 1998, would he have still done so? Answers not required. Remember: context is everything.

CHAPTER 7

PUBLIC PRIVACY

'No one ever went broke underestimating the intelligence of the great masses of the plain people' (often misquoted as 'intelligence of the American people'). At least, that was the view of the American journalist and literary critic HL Mencken (1880–1956). He despaired of the tabloids' spike in popularity during the mid-1920s. Mencken himself wrote for the much more respectable *Chicago Tribune*, which has outlasted more than a few tabloids. The substance of tabloids back in the 1920s was tamer than it is today, but lurid and sensational stories dominated then as they do now. And today, we have tabloid television shows and internet sites as complements.

Mencken could only recognize the growth of tabloid culture in the USA. Today, he would have seen it everywhere on Planet Earth. The Kardashians are, as we know, both products and producers of tabloid culture. They emerged from an environment in which malicious gossip, scandalous relationships and transgressions that bring dishonor, disgrace and infamy are parts of the daily menu of news. The kind of publication that anguished Mencken was actually quite decorous compared to those that followed in the 1950s. The magazine that broke with the decorum and offered a template for the later scandal sheets was *Confidential*, which launched in December 1952, and which, according to *Inside the Hollywood Fan Magazine* author Anthony Slide, 'revealed [stars] in all their scandalous modes, without apology and without restraint.'

It was one of a number of publications that provided gossip, hearsay and miscellaneous tittle-tattle, mainly on Hollywood actors. The so-called 'golden age of Hollywood' (1930s and 1940s) was over and the lifestyles of the people associated with the film industry were fair game for gossip columnists. *Confidential*'s importance lay less in its own content – though it '"devastated the private lives of hundreds of celebrities," as entertainment journalist Victor Davis wrote in 2002 – more in its wider effects. "Other publications, magazines and tabloids, were emboldened to venture further than they'd ever gone before in printing scabrous material," reported Davis. His use of the adjective scabrous suggests that content became sensational, indecent – at least by 1950s standards – and, unlike the neat and elegant stories sanctioned by the studios, rough. Several other similarly uninhibited publications followed.'

In the 1950s, scandals could and often did prove to be ruinous for Hollywood stars. In those days, singers and other artists with ambitions would aim to transfer to movies. Sinatra, Elvis and practically every other singer of international renown had designs on La La Land. It became a treacherous place once gossip magazines started hunting for prey. They were all responding to the spicy palate cultivated by *Confidential*. Plain people, as Mencken called them, were changing: they demanded more than fabulous images of extraordinary people with remarkable lives: they wanted narratives – real stories of people they could recognize and perhaps relate to as human beings with the same kinds of strengths and weaknesses as themselves. They wanted to learn of histories, events or, even better, chronicles that conveyed a moral lesson about what's right and wrong, prudent or foolhardy and which gave them license to judge. They wanted to engage.

We can assume readers of such material found it irresistible, in the same way we find gross-out films irresistible: foul-mouth dialogue, gale-force slapstick and gags about defecation, erectile dysfunction, and other bodily matters; but we go with the flow. And, it seems, they weren't embarrassed about reading tittle-tattle. Though they probably would have been if the stories were as revelatory and candid as they are today. It's easy to imagine the response of readers of the 1950s to an exposé that purported to disclose the dirty little secrets of, say, Bette Davis. 'I'm an admirer of Miss Davis and enjoy watching her play strong independent characters in films such as *Dangerous* and *All About Eve*,' a fan might have remarked. 'But her private life is of no concern to me and I have no interest in learning about aspects of her that she would properly regard as personal.' It was believable in the 1950s, but barely conceivable today.

Tastes and sensibilities were changing. So fast, in fact, that in 1961, a professor of anthropology at City University of New York, published the results of a study of readers of *Confidential*. By the time of Charles Winick's original research (between 1954 and 1957), sales of the magazine, which sold at a quarter, were running at 4.1 million copies per issue, and Winick wanted to 'determine the reasons for the unprecedented success of the magazine.'

He thought that, while 'the general public has always been interested in the private life of celebrities,' the relative prosperity of the 1950s had 'in some way' helped 'to unleash feelings of guilt which could express themselves by reading about celebrities who had sinned.'

If we ignore for a moment Winick's explanation of the sources and functions of the curiosity and his use of the word 'sinned,' his basic suspicions seemed justified. *Confidential* magazine was making a frontal assault on the celebrity system. Winick meant that the publication was challenging Hollywood's well-practised system of crushing any attempt by journalists to expose details of actors' or directors' private lives. *Confidential* focused on 'the sins and sex of the mighty.' As do countless magazines today.

'Realizing that the celebrity was an ordinary mortal with human failings' fortified readers. I'm not sure if Winick was joking, but, even if he were, he captured the typical response of readers perfectly: 'We can't be so bad if they're doing the things they do.' It must have eased the guilt felt when prying into others' lives. This was 1961, remember. Color tv wasn't even around. So Winick's depiction of readers exorcizing themselves vicariously is a plausible explanation of how the magazine was able to command such a formidable readership. *Confidential* was probably exploiting either a new curiosity, or, if we go with Winick's argument, an old curiosity that was being expressed through a newer medium. But we'd be naïve if we didn't realize *Confidential* also fertilized that curiosity. (The magazine's stopped publication in 1978 after its founding proprietor died.)

Fans wanted a fresco of the glamor and opulence of Hollywood, not a mirror of reality. They knew what they wanted from Hollywood stars. They wanted faces of hypnotic beauty, like those of Grace Kelly or Hedy Lamarr and impossibly perfect bodies clothed in the most exclusive gowns. They wanted to believe these celestial beings were halfway to the heavens, not condemned to the tedious repetition of ordinary life. They knew what they wanted: piquant details delivered with immediacy and without the purifying filter of journalists, less still Hollywood publicists.

If Hollywood wanted a story slaughtered at birth, *Confidential* flew to the slaughter ground and tried to rescue it. Its sales suggest it succeeded in great measure. Its grubbing often produced stories that made Hollywood's untouchable characters seem like the magnificent idol of Nebuchadnezzar's dream, with feet 'part of iron and part of clay.' In other words, they were flawed, just like everyone else.

Try pronouncing judgment on the apparent misbehavior of someone you know, or think you know – or would like to know. It's a pleasant surprise: quite a satisfying experience. 'Disgraceful!' 'Bravo!' 'Shame on you!' 'Good for you!' Whatever conclusion we reach, there's a payoff. Not even Winick, weaponized with his research, ventured a guess about whether the editors of *Confidential* and other magazine actually intended their readers to judge the figures they wrote about. But they certainly insinuated those readers into a moral discourse. Winick wrote about 'a kind of magical control over the famous and a vehicle for hostility against them, concealed behind expressions of morality and surprise.' I think this works even today: fans enjoy being able to judge the people they saw – and still see – on screens. While the tabloids, film quarterlies and the other publications that flourished in the mid-twentieth century exposed the dubious conduct of stars and the epigones who tried to emulate them, there was abundant source material on which to base judgment.

Years later, Kim Kardashian reversed the earlier trend: instead of concealing her deeds, she pushed them out to audience, each story virtually granting audiences authority to make evaluations of her. Kardashian was mindful of her own very obvious human flaws, even if the ones of which she seemed most aware were physical ones. Her fate, such as it was, was to be of all-consuming interest to similarly flawed human beings, who didn't just respect, envy and worship her; they judged her.

So here was a woman who probably gave audiences more sex, nudity and assorted other raw material than they could have wished for. It was almost impossible to resist judging her. 'What I learned from the media and will never repeat' was not a sentence likely to leave Kardashian's lips. In 2014, for example, and for no apparent reason (not even money), the then mother-of-one posed covered in oil, wearing nothing but black opera gloves, earrings and several pearl chokers, for the cover of *PAPER* magazine. As I related in Chapter 4, Kardashian, for the same shoot, had another photograph taken in a sparkly black dress and a champagne glass balancing on her behind, which she was sticking out to make a kind of an impromptu human shelf. (She was still wearing the opera gloves.)

Why would anyone, at least anyone who wasn't abjectly desperate for money, expose themselves to condemnation, derision and disapproval? Kardashian must have realized she would be ridiculed on grounds of taste. But that was the point. As soon as people stopped pronouncing judgement on her, she was on her way to celebrities' *Ultima Thule*. Kardashian offered herself as an exquisitely modern version of the reprobates who were, in medieval times, secured by hands and feet in those wooden structures called stocks and exposed to public mockery or assault.

Think of the episodes that invited public appraisal: the 72-day marriage in 2011 (and they said it would never last); the revenge on Taylor Swift that earned her the sobriquet 'the Sun Tzu of social media' from Amy Zimmerman (Sun Tzu was the 4th century BC military strategist and author of *The Art of War*); the robbery in Paris when Kim was bound, gagged and robbed at gunpoint before being relieved of jewelry valued at $11 million. Kim's Instagram video in 2018 triggered a comment from Khloé, 'She's anorexic here,' which, in turn prompted outrage and a global debate about eating disorders.

The family also were involved in various legal battles, which hit the headlines, especially the one that started in 2013 when the *Daily Mail* reported that the Kardashian sisters' Khroma beauty line had been pulled from stores after they were sued for stealing the name from another line, KROMA. The suit was settled in 2014. Since then the family has been regularly hit with lawsuits. As *Vanity Fair*'s Lauren Le Vine pronounced in 2017, 'The more famous they get, the more legal battles they face. It comes with the territory.'

The Kardashian-inspired dilemmas, paradoxes and conundrums were mostly tragicomic, but it would be ungenerous to call them contrived. The family just seems to venture into areas that we'd all like to be in, but are glad we're not. This is not quite as self-contradictory as it sounds. Few people consciously want to live a Kardashian lifestyle, though many of us are curious and, while jewelry of the kind favored by Kim might be the height of extravagant vulgarity, many would like a pair of earrings from her collection, if only to pay off the mortgage, purchase a second home or so in the Caribbean, buy a Lamborghini and start thinking about whether a helicopter would be more convenient than a Lear Jet. And we can still moan about the ostentatiousness of KK's jewelry.

Judging is fulfilling. It makes us think, which is always a good start. Because there's a moral involved, we have to decide what's right and wrong, or, more likely, the rightest or wrongest. The inner wrestling is rendered painless by the simple fact that our verdict has no consequences of note for the people involved and is, as far as we're concerned, inconsequential. Perhaps we've always done this and, today, we're merely replicating an age-old practice. But we do it openly and without embarrassment, as if we are eavesdropping mediators in private conversations. There's no guilt attached.

That's show business, isn't it? Some readers will undoubtedly assume that the interface of entertainment and blather has always been like a boundary between two liquids that swish together and nowadays emulsify. After all, show business thrives and has always thrived off buzz, that sense of excitement about or interest in someone. The media have always either reflected, or more probably generated the buzz. Word-of-mouth is the greatest transmitter though.

Kim probably prides herself on her ability to rile and divide. Half the world, it seems, regards her as vacuous, superficial, facile, insubstantial and ignorant, an apotheosis of style without content. The other half treasures her. We all admire the cheek and chic of how whatever she does gets done. And we all must, at some time, have wondered why anyone thought it was worth doing.

Suppose, in 1986, you dreamt up an idea for a TV show and pitched it to a media executive you knew. He (in the mid-1980s, it was bound to be a man) listens carefully before laughing in your face. 'Get lost! Who in their right minds would want to watch a bunch of losers screaming at each other about who is screwing whose wife and has knocked up somebody's daughter?' You think a while and tell him you think it could be sold as potentially therapeutic, a kind of televised rehab. He's not convinced: 'You stand no chance, absolutely no chance at persuading anybody to sit in front of cameras and 'fess up millions that his wife has been giving oral sex to paying customers, then blowing the proceeds to score oxycodone for her and her lesbian girlfriend.' Jerry Springer had answers to both questions. Somehow, he managed to persuade USA Networks Studios to make the show. It launched in 1991. Within seven years, it had become the fastest growing TV show in syndication ever, surpassing Oprah's all-conquering daytime talk show.

Ostensibly, *The Jerry Springer Show* tried to repair dysfunctional relationships by inviting the parties to said relationships to talk through their issues. The parties involved were often members of homo-, hetero-, and bisexual love triangles (sometimes rectangles). Transsexuals and hermaphrodites shared space with others who regarded themselves as straight. Sex, religion, mid-life crises, more sex – they were all up for discussion. Audiences devoured it, though not merely as consumers; given half-the chance, most would have gladly leapt onto the stage and divulged their innermost secrets in front of 10 million others (that was the peak US viewing audience in 1998). Springer's show was frequently amusing, in much the same way as a whoopee cushion. It encouraged open exchange about private affairs and bodily matters. The concern with dysfunctional relationships was the organizing principle. If it were a Rorschach test, critics would have seen a shapeless splotch. Audiences, on the other hand, must have seen a keyhole shaped pattern. Erin St John Kelly, of the *New York Times*, wrote in response: 'Elitists are out of touch, and he [Springer] gives viewers a show with some meaning to them.'

It's a persuasive comment and I'll expand it. Looking back, the show presented a version of what we'd now call a chatroom in which depressives talk about episodes in their life and others are so amused, they're induced to share their own experiences, knowing full well others will find them amusing. It was a coherent reflection of a society in which no one felt inhibited by the presence of strangers. In fact, everyone seemed empowered by the opportunity to share their experiences. Looking back, it probably had a strong claim to being the most sociologically insightful TV show in history at that point, even if it was mainly about quarrelling. The curiosity that kept viewers rapt was probably veering on the prurient; but, by the 1990s, voyeurism was almost respectable. When sociology professor Frank Furedi wrote, 'The act of "sharing" – turning private troubles into public stories – is now deeply embedded in popular culture,' he was recognizing our appetites for devouring those stories.

'A confessional culture critically depends not just on subjects who are willing to tell all, but also on the presence of an audience that regards revelations as entertainment,' wrote gender studies professor Juliet Williams in 2006. This prompts a question: would the Kardashians have happened in a time and place where other people's private lives were not entertaining? The answer is, of course, no. This probably sounds more disturbing than it is; but it doesn't mean we're spiritually and morally bankrupt; it means our conception of privacy has changed.

Over 4,000 miles away from the studio in Chicago where Springer's show was shot, a Dutch TV producer must have been peering at the screen and wondering: 'What comes after this?' John de Mols would have probably realized that people were becoming unselfconscious and quite relaxed about talking in public about episodes in their lives that would make audiences blush (although the audiences were more likely to sit agog with curiosity or laugh out loud). A thought could have flashed across De Mols' mind: what if you could induce people not only to talk about their private lives, but actually conduct their private lives in front of cameras? De Mols, a partner of a Netherlands-based TV production company, probably didn't know the exact answer; but he must have had a hunch. And thus *Big Brother* was conceived.

The format of what we now call reality TV had been around since at least 1992, when MTV introduced *The Real World*, and possibly as far back as 1973, if we include PBS's *An American*

Family, which was a nascent form of the genre. *Big Brother*'s uniqueness was its timing; its premise of interning people in a house and setting them tasks, while viewers voted on who they wanted to evict would have suited one of those psychological obedience experiments of the 1960s. But in 1999, when nosiness was newly respectable, it was made for TV. And, of course, audiences weren't asked to sit back in respectful astonishment; they effectively became part of the narrative as it unwound (a bit like those experimenters who administered the electric shocks to noncompliant participants in the Milgram studies of the 1960s). It was interactive television before even the internet had become properly interactive. Audiences might not have realized it at the time, but change was going on; the age-old division between performers and spectators was in revision.

Big Brother was first to exploit this, but, in 2009, *Jersey Shore* wrung it dry. The MTV show dispensed with many of the more gimmicky elements of other reality shows and featured eight young Italian Americans, all as tanned, toned and 'back-sack-and-crack' waxed as each other. Their pursuit of the good life was the subject matter of the program. Some advertisers, including Domino's Pizza and Dell Computers, pulled their commercials following the debut episode, objecting to the cultural stereotype of Italian Americans. The ignoble adventures of the pleasure-seekers and their unfathomable ignorance enraged many critics; the show was, in many people's eyes, the nadir of cultural abasement. 'It makes *Big Brother* look like Dostoyevsky,' fumed Andrew Clark, of the *Guardian* (July 27, 2010). (It wasn't an unfair comparison: the Russian master revealed insights about the religious, political and moral problems posed by human suffering.)

Jersey Shore became MTV's most successful show ever, with 8.4 million viewers. The audience grew after cast-member Nicole 'Snooki' Polizzi was punched in the face during the taping of an early episode. Someone must have joined the dots: feature aspects of human behavior that people find nauseating or repugnant and viewing figures rise. The association was mediated by traditional newspapers and broadcasters, which bristled at the denigration, while MTV regaled viewers with the honest accounts of ordinary people's lives. Polizzi went on to a rewarding career outside the show, as did practically every member. A couple of journalism professors coined the 'Snooki Effect' to describe the ways in watching reality TV influences audience's perceptions of how, in particular, young women behave. Karyn Riddle and JJ De Simone's research found that viewers' beliefs about how much women gossiped and argued were 'cultivated' by watching programs like *Jersey Shore*.

The success of *Jersey Shore* and its British equivalent, *Geordie Shore*, which followed in 2011, provides an index to changing sensibilities. Entertainment can enlighten, inform and edify, and it can poke, disturb and annoy. There's no paradox and, if there is, it's more likely Nietzschean than Dostoyevskian; we decide for ourselves what we like, rather than rely on others to dictate to us. Audiences inured to the raw and relatable drama of reality TV ignored, or perhaps defied, the disapproval of critics.

There's no doubting the dominant medium of the past 70 or so years. Television is like a life form that descended to earth in the middle of twentieth century and proceeded to change all other life forms. As public fascination with the lives of others has grown, so TV has both cultivated and chronicled our sensibility and guided us into territories that would have been taboo outside the twenty-first century. Thanks to TV, audiences were turned into guiltless eavesdroppers on private lives. Of course, if you probe too much on private lives, there comes a point at which they cease to be private and, after that, the concept of privacy itself becomes uncertain.

> *'I think whatshername is a total bitch for what she did ...'*

> *'I pretend I'm friendly with so-and-so, but, in truth, I can't stand him because ...'*

We keep private thoughts like these to ourselves, or perhaps share them with a small and select group of others on the presumption that they will go no further. At least we *used* to. Springer and the many variations of reality shows that followed Big Brother disclosed an emerging truth: the state of not being available for public attention was changing — privacy was not what it used to be. It used to be important to keep and element of what once passed as a private life to ourselves; we respected and protected a distinction between what we did and said openly and what we thought and felt to ourselves. By the time *The Anna Nicole Show* debuted on E! in 2002, viewers of confessional and reality shows were habituated to overhearing others' conversations, particularly ones that involved intimate secrets. (The story surrounding the E! show opened Chapter 1.)

Springer had many imitators: shows that purported to offer guidance to people with personal problems were effectively acknowledgements that ordinary people, not celebrities, were enthusiastic about talking openly about matters that, a few years before, would have been regarded as strictly confidential. People talked openly about shameful matters, while others were willing to listen to them and relish the experience. Some shows, in particular the UK's *Jeremy Kyle Show*, were taken off air in spring 2019, after one of its featured guests appeared to have committed suicide. Reality shows were the equivalent of peepholes; viewers were invited to look through an aperture, if only for the duration of the program. A better analogy is the mutoscope, a gadget popular in the early 1900s. Consumers would drop a coin in a slot and look through a peephole at a short film, one of the most popular being *What the Butler Saw*, depicting what the prying servant would see if he were gaping through a keyhole at the lady of the house while she was undressing. This type of entertainment lost popularity in the 1930s when filmed pornography caught on.

Any reader old enough to remember television at the start of the 1990s will know how unthinkable it would have been to switch on in the middle of the afternoon and find a grown man discussing his premature ejaculation, or a woman freely talking about her MtF trans girlfriend. These would have been strictly personal and unambiguously private matters. But, by the early 2000s, they were the kind of subjects that were aired every day on several TV shows. And, if I can segue briefly, I should add that privacy has never been static; like everything else in our social world, it's subject to continual change. For example, Italy's paparazzi started taking an uncommonly salacious interest in the lives of the rich and famous in the 1960s. Curiously, audiences found their stories and pictures quite rewarding. They could praise, damn or just tut-tut over others' behavior while they read their morning paper.

The arrival of Twitter in 2006 could hardly have been better timed. It appeared on the landscape at the exact moment in history when people were shrugging off any residual guilt about wanting to peer into other people's lives. Twitter didn't exactly allow them to peer, but it delivered short snippets of information, often quite personal information, and people could just enjoy or, more likely, react — often by sharing snippets of their own. Twitter enabled users to share with specific groups of others, but with the potential to reach anyone else who used the social network. The original concept might have been to let people send words that were as inconsequential as the sound of chirruping birds, but it soon developed into the gossip medium par excellence. It also became a potent marketing instrument for celebrities to tout practically anything, as I noted in Chapter 5.

I have no idea whether anyone on earth, including the people who conceived of Twitter, could have anticipated how tempting the medium would become. There was nothing in the design of the Twitter that enticed users into sharing confidential information. Users weren't coaxed, as they were on the TV shows. They weren't offered prizes, or any kind of reward at all: they chose to disclose more about themselves than anyone expected. Perhaps Twitter functioned as a purgatory. I don't mean it was a place of suffering or torment for those wishing to expiate their sins in a last ditch attempt to get to heaven (if it were Charles Winick would have recommended it to the subjects of *Confidential*). But it was a channel with a kind of cleansing property – users were allowed to release whatever information they wished and with impunity, within reason. It had a sort of self-perpetuating manner. I mean by this that, candid tweets prompted recipients to respond with candor themselves. And it seems the lack of inhibition had a purifying effect. At least, that's one way of understanding the baffling rise of twitter.

Readers might be thinking privacy, at least privacy in the traditional sense of the condition, has gone. You don't have to search far for evidence: on public transport, people discuss their affairs without compunction, often leaving the speakerphone on so that other passengers can hear both ends of the conversation. Twitter is now part of the natural order of things. Instagram, Snapchat and WhatsApp have added impudence and brio, making sharing arguably the defining experience of our time. We share money, knowledge and hours and hours of our time; it would be untenable to ask people not to share what used to pass as a private life. Is this a bad thing?

It seems only a few years ago that privacy shielded all manner of vile practices that are now in the common domain. Child abuse was hushed-up. Domestic violence was secreted as an internal family issue. Women were often persuaded they were partly responsible if they were raped. People with developmental disorders, such as Asperger syndrome, seldom revealed, less still, discussed their experiences. These are some of the one-time private matters that have been turned into social affairs. People who were at one time marginalized as sexual minorities or worse, have been emboldened to make their predilections and identities public without inhibition. The kind of cultural fluidity that has streamed through this book wouldn't have been possible with a protective screen of privacy.

Since *Big Brother* started in 1999 *(The Anna Nicole Show* followed in 2002, *Jersey Shore* would start in 2009), reality shows have been uniformly panned by critics and loved by audiences. It's not possible to make sense of the oceanic cultural change of the 2000s without respecting their impact. Accompanied by the equally influential social media (Facebook and Twitter launched in 2004 and 2006 respectively), reality TV effectively dismantled notions of privacy and gave licence to distribute thoughts, knowledge, emotions, images and any other kind of meme without considering the receivers.

The days when celebrities could operate by-the-numbers were gone. Anyone who ventured into the public domain with a mind to become famous had to strike a bargain: surrender what you used to call a private life or go back to obscurity. Audiences were as entitled to know as much about the people they followed as they were prepared to divulge about themselves. Notice how I didn't write '*feel* as entitled.' Today's audiences don't just sense they have licence to explore the people they relate to 360 degrees. Public privacy confers authority on the people who are supposed by many to be celebrity culture's chumps.

Celebrities are pretty much like everybody else today: candid, open, prepared to discuss their weight issues, botched nose jobs, failed marriages, dreams about babies, and sex in unusual places. Audiences might once have been respectful but powerless, denied access to anything but the contrived personae celebrities wanted them to see. Now, they expect unrestricted admission and celebs are obliged to respond. In the process, they reveal themselves as ordinary flesh-and-blood mortals with the same kinds of vulnerabilities and proneness to errors as everyone else. This used to infuriate many commentators who denounced the generation of celebrities born of reality TV as merely famous for being famous, as if that were a disgrace.

The popular assumption used to be that fame, whether sourced from notoriety or triumph, had to be achieved rather than assigned. Actually, it's *always* been assigned; audiences do the assigning. For military heroes, prominent politicians, inventors and, to a lesser extent, artists, fame would have been unimaginable without their accomplishments. But the state of being known by many is a social relationship; in other words, the crucial determinant of fame is not the accomplishment or even the person who accomplished it, but the people who recognize them both. Fame is always a matter of attribution rather than achievement. Plain people (as Mencken called them), with nothing extraordinary to boast of, nor any discernible capacity beyond being relatable, establish themselves in our collective consciousness. Then they're famous.

So where does this leave talent? In the 2000s, critics scratched their heads and wondered why talent-lite wannabes on reality TV shows captivated audiences. And the answer stared straight back at them: they were ordinary. Unlike the untouchable, inaccessible and slightly inhuman stars of the twentieth century, inmates of the Big Brother house or other reality shows resembled the audience. They might be unpleasant and their lives might be trite; but they had some passion, a little wit and a will to live. Just like the people who watched them.

I wrote earlier about how Paris Hilton created the template for aspiring celebrities seeking to channel their talents, but without ever knowing what those talents were, or even if they existed. The suffocating formal constraints of having to act, sing, dance or cruise elegantly on the catwalk were lifted in the early years of the century. As long as interested audiences wanted to follow her exploits and effectively commission the media to operate as their proxy, then all she had to do was appear. The only talent required was relatability, a noun that's cropped up throughout this book. After Hilton, *Big Brother* and the miscellaneous reality shows that brought audiences actively into the narrative, talent took on a new meaning. It was whatever audiences decided.

Talent has never been something that people possess: it's whatever we acknowledge. If we spot someone in a reality show whom we like or hate, or tends to provoke in us a sensation we find agreeable and keeps us watching, then we can legitimately conclude that figure has a talent. Reality TV didn't kill off the traditional twentieth-century celebrity; but it allowed audiences to build their own kind of celebrities, ones that looked and behaved like them. Whether they liked or hated the new characters was interesting but irrelevant;

not so interesting, but crucially relevant was whether they provoked audiences in a way they found rewarding. If they did, audiences took notice, and endowed them with a certain talent.

Before readers shudder at this approach to talent, let me pretend we could jump aboard the DeLorean from Chapter 6, and take Rihanna back 600 years, stand her on a stage and ask her to perform. Would bystanders be impressed? No, not before microphones had been invented. Now we gasp at her awesomeness. We can appreciate her because we live in an age in which her style of pop music is valued. By contrast, Francesco Canova da Milano (1497–1543) was one of the greatest lute players of the Renaissance period. Would he be acclaimed today? Like beauty, talent is in the eye of the beholder: not so much a gift, but an agreement. (A lute is an egg-shaped string instrument, played by plucking.)

Audiences are ruthless in the way they adopt, adore and discard celebrities. They're just as much products of their culture as the people they follow; every generation is initiated into a world loaded with values, common ways of looking at life and limits or controls. These are literally inescapable. They change continually. Our tastes never stay the same.

Audiences once accepted that the glamorous, almost godlike stars were complexly different from the everyday fans. But the surveillance ushered in, at first, by scandal-seeking entertainers like Madonna then everyone who aspired to fame, gave audiences access to a new kind of entertainment – prying.

Hilton was a *succès de scandal* waiting to happen. One can imagine Madonna's response when she heard about Hilton's notorious sex tape of 2003: 'Damn! Why didn't I think of that?' Hilton may not have had the common touch, but she had some unmistakably human faults and more than

her fair share of fashion faux pas, romantic disasters, fake
tan mishaps and accidental losses (she once mislaid a $2m
engagement ring). She was even stopped from boarding a
flight to Australia due to an invalid passport. And, of course,
she was in a reality show from 2003 to 2007.

Hilton's theatrical extravagance was an echo of previous
decades, but her clumsiness and ineffectual forays into traditional areas of show business were premonitory. Audiences
delighted in their new, unwholesome but thoroughly enjoyable ability to mock and, with the arrival of an interactive
internet, share their glee. Antagonistic critics of the early
2000s were right: the famous-for-being-famous types were a
disfiguring and unwelcome presence on the cultural landscape. I can't be sure, but I imagine doomsayers greeted television with the same invective. Radio too. Even Johannes
Gutenberg's fifteenth-century contraption that eventually
made printed books possible would have probably been
received with suspicion. Artists, from Dali to the Beatles,
Joyce to Duchamp, Lynch to Reich (Steve, this time; not
Wilhelm), have at some point been deplored. They all issued
challenges. Reality TV and the particular epoch it represented
do the same.

In responding so certainly and effusively audiences effectively created reality TV. In turn, it changed them; coaxed
along by the complementary force of social media, audiences
found the insight into the lives of others delectable. It wasn't
just gawping and listening; it was the exchange of opinions,
the deliberations on rightness and wrongness and the expressions of love and malice that made the whole experience so
satisfying. It's probably irreversible; we'll never reestablish a
hard-and-fast distinction between public and private spheres
again. In truth, the division was probably never as rigid as it
seems in hindsight, anyway. The very fact that we're social
animals, gregarious, companionable and expressive makes

sharing inevitable. Like any other major art form, television never stopped poking us: 'Wake up! You might find this tasteless, crass and excessive. But give it a try.' Our reaction was something like: 'It is tasteless and, yes, it's crass alright. Is it excessive? No. We'll have some more.' They got it.

CHAPTER 8

LEVERAGED FAME

Culture is always at the mercy of serendipity. In 2007, a series of discoveries and unrelated incidents intersected, or perhaps collided, to change history. E!'s new reality show *Keeping Up With the Kardashians*, received poor reviews, though its rating were boosted by Kim Kardashian's appearances in an online sex tape, in February, and on the cover of *Playboy*, in December. In June, Apple released its iPhone, a device that allowed users to watch films, listen to music and browse the net as well as take photographs and make phone calls. Twitter's online microblogging service that enabled computer users to distribute short messages to groups of followers all day and all night had been available for a while but spiked sharply from March. And Paris Hilton, then one of the best-known people in the world, was jailed for 45 days after being found guilty of violating her probation for a drink-driving conviction. The result was an improbable but potent constellation. The pattern still dictates the way we live.

Kylie Jenner was 10 in 2007. The daughter of Kris Jenner (who was previously married to OJ Simpson's lawyer Robert

Kardashian, who died in 2003) and Caitlyn Jenner (previously, Bruce Jenner), she grew up surrounded by her sisters Kim, Khloé, Kourtney and Kendall, and brother Robert, in front of E!'s cameras. In early 2019 the business magazine *Forbes* reported she had become the youngest self-made billionaire ever. (Kim, then 37, by comparison, was worth just $350 million.)

If you thought the story of Kim's rise to fame was preposterous and farfetched, you should probably sit down, if you're not already doing so, and take a Xanax before learning how her half-sister conquered the world (or at least started on her path to becoming the youngest billionaire in history). Both stories offer reflections on how we live today. But before I get to Kylie, let me ask what might seem a superfluous question: why would anyone want to be famous?

Is it so attractive in itself? Or is it the means to an end? The end in question could be a life crammed with consumer goods and an endless supply of luxuries. The kind of life the Kardashians appear to have. Maybe it isn't just about commodities and luxury, so much as influence: there's satisfaction in knowing millions of people are going to hang on to your every word, so that, if you recommend an appetite suppressant (as Khloé did in 2018) then others will accept your advice without question. There is still money in it; being an influencer, as we noticed in Chapter 5, is one of the most effective methods of accumulating serious amounts of money in the shortest period of time.

Or maybe it's the adulation. No, make that the *adoration* of people, who don't just admire, respect or even venerate famous figures, but sometimes actually worship them occasionally in bizarre ways. Like the guy who broke into Taylor Swift's New York townhouse, had a shower and took a nap in her bed, but didn't steal anything. The intruder was arrested but must have budgeted for that: his recompense was a few hours in repose among his idol's accoutrements. Most celebs have got past the point at which they used to pretend the paparazzi were smothering them and scream, 'If this kind of fame is heaven, show me the way to hell!' Nobody believed them, anyway.

I imagine being regarded with affection bordering on deification is a priority, though not one celebrities wish to acknowledge. Fame often begets more fame, if only because the media does the begetting. And it often begets admiration. Who doesn't luxuriate in being admired? The rise of social media has made fame a sort of meritocracy in which people compete for the admiration of others. People are selected according to merit; in other words, if audiences think you deserve fame, you get it.

Expressed like this, wanting or craving fame and the esteem it brings seems perfectly reasonable. Until, you think about someone like Pedro Ruiz. He was prepared to work hard for fame. If not fame, a degree of attention. If not attention, the awareness that he existed. Hard enough to try a terrific stunt that would earn him recognition, possibly from around the world.

Ruiz and his partner Monalisa Perez, a 19-year-old from Halstad, Minnesota, were habitual vloggers on YouTube. They'd pull maneuvers and play pranks on each other, such as putting spicy hot chili in each other's sandwiches or baby powder as icing sugar on doughnuts. Pedro's other antics included jumping into the swimming pool from the top of a house, no hesitation. A self-accredited adrenaline junkie, Ruiz also posted on Facebook videos of himself chasing storms.

He'd like his efforts to look easy and breezy, but there was a grim determination and ingenuity in his work, and it *was* work. Audiences don't just pop out of a vacuum, not even on YouTube: Ruiz worked hard for his fans, so hard they could almost hear and feel the strain. It's difficult to carp about someone who wanted to please the audience as much as Ruiz. On the evening of June 26, 2017, Monalisa, then 19, tweeted: 'Me and Pedro are probably going to shoot one of the most dangerous videos ever. HIS idea not MINE.'

Fame-seeking daredevil Ruiz set up one camera on the back of a vehicle and another camera on a ladder nearby. 'Imagine when we have 300,000 subscribers,' Perez said to the camera before aiming a 0.50-caliber Desert Eagle pistol at Ruiz standing about a foot (0.3 meters) away. He was holding a hardcover encyclopedia to his chest, his – and we presume Perez's – assumption being that the bullet would not pass through the thick tome. In the event, it did. Ruiz died at the scene from a single gunshot wound to the chest. He was 22.

Perez was pregnant with the couple's second child at the time of the shooting; she was charged with second-degree manslaughter in the shooting of her boyfriend. She posted $7,000 cash bail and was released. Six months later, she pleaded guilty to the charge and was given a six-month prison sentence.

When asked by a reporter from WDAY-TV in Fargo about the incident, an aunt of Ruiz's revealed: 'He had told me about that idea and I said, "Don't do it. Don't do it. Why are you going to use a gun? Why?"' He answered: 'Because we want more viewers. *We want to get famous.*'

The reply was simultaneously foolish and logical; like the response of someone about to climb on an amusement park ride that's been declared faulty. They might say: 'Everybody rides the safe ones; no one takes notice of them.'

Kylie Jenner didn't need to risk killing herself for the sake of a few million more followers. She had over 110 million followers on Instagram and 25 million more on Twitter; and that's before Snapchat. She grew up as a reality TV star and, as far as we know, had no ambitions to become a recording artist, screen actor, writer, or supermodel. Makeup was her thing. Kylie Cosmetics launched in 2016 with a $29 'lip kit,' comprising a set of lipstick and lip liner. But, of course, she's a Kardashian. That means that she advertises. By 'advertises,' I mean endorses, licences, promotes and, in several other ways, influences consumers to buy products such as Puma footwear and PacSun clothing. And along the way this made her a billionaire.

Ultimately her fortune, like that of Kim, the rest of the family, derived from one place; the same place where Ruiz sought his fame; the same place where anyone with aspirations to be famous needs to be; the same place billions visit every day. 'Social media is an amazing platform,' enthused Jenner. 'I have such easy access to my fans and my customers.' The two are interchangeable: fans *are* customers.

The preposterous aspect of Kylie's story is that, in 2014 – before she formed her company – she inadvertently (I think) underlined a truism that runs through the various arguments of this book like a neurotransmitter through the brain's neurons (in other words, it jumps across the gaps). That is: scandal is now a valuable resource. Kylie's wasn't a scandal to compare with sex tapes, lewdness in public places, S&M on stage, or any of the various other disreputable adventures covered elsewhere in these pages. In fact, on reflection, it's a bit anodyne. Perhaps that's what makes Kylie's ascent all the more preposterous: the size of her lips appeared enlarged – sorry, were enlarged – when she appeared in a picture posted on Instagram. 'As with sister Kim's sex-tape fame, Kylie Cosmetics got started by capitalizing on a scandal,' wrote Natalie Robehmed of *Forbes*, on July 11, 2018.

For reasons that are best understood inside the rational universe of young women, especially the millions who follow

Kylie, this created a viral discourse and a craze that was known as the 'Kylie Jenner Lip Challenge.' This involved pursing the lips, pushing them into an empty shot glass, then sucking in; the suction stimulated bloodflow to the lips causing a temporary swelling. Not just swelling, but bruising and other unwanted effects. The significance of the outrage Kylie had inadvertently provoked merely by posting a picture wasn't lost on mother and momager Kris: the lip kits went on sale in 2015, all the marketing done online. Kylie brought in e-commerce platform Shopify. The first batch sold out before you could refresh the page. A product that was selling initially for under $30 was soon going for $1000 on eBay. Within months the lip kits had transformed into Kylie Cosmetics, which diversified into over 50 products and turned over more than $300m in its first year.

The volatility of celebrity culture means that any company synonymous with a single figure will slump just as surely as the currency of the celeb plummets. Paris Hilton is no longer the commanding presence she once was; nor are the products with which she is associated. Ditto Kate Moss. It's possible that, had the stricken Pedro Ruiz lived, he could have monetized his YouTube fame by endorsing products or even, like Kylie, launching his own. It's unlikely that he could have sustained it, though.

On the other hand, maybe Ruiz just wanted to be watched and have his name remembered, if only for a short period. It may sound reductive and one-dimensional, and I have no evidence to give heft to my proposition, but I sense the Ruiz approach to fame is slipping as the Kylie model gains traction. 'Jenner understood how fame can be leveraged,' Robehmed detected. Leverage can be used in a number of ways; in this context, I think Robehmed meant Jenner used her renown to maximum effect in the market (as in, for example, 'Disney has been able to leverage its arsenal of

Marvel, Pixar, and *Star Wars* movies to extract better terms from cinema chains').

Fame, from this perspective, isn't an end state people are aiming at; it's a means of getting other scarce resources, like money or privilege. Political power is another scarce resource. Many politicians use social media, often provocatively, to attract attention or to crowdsource opinion. Robehmed pointed out that both Kylie Jenner and Donald Trump, who was elected President of the US in 2016, were products of reality TV shows. 'They are as much brands as people,' she maintains. 'Fame is just another word for free marketing.'

Think how many people currently on the radar started in reality shows. Were they all hungry for fame? Likely. But they soon learned that, when a nightclub offers $1500–$3000 to show up for a couple of hours, and a fake tan company pays them thousands to post approving messages on social media, then being famous becomes a job, a way of earning a living. Not exactly hand-to-mouth either. The vagaries of today's celebrity culture mean that this kind of leveraged fame is inevitably conditional, and, while it's difficult to imagine how any of the Kardashians, Taylor Swift or many of their A-list peers could ever be *unfamed* (so to speak), graduates of reality TV or talent shows are always liable to be endangered species. That doesn't alter the market possibilities; companies, particularly those with young consumer bases are driven forcefully by social media influencers. Kylie, in 2018–19, was in a league of her own.

———

In 2009, *USA Today*'s Anne Oldenburg mused that 'the moral to the 2000 decade story' was 'the growth of reality television, celebrity bloggers and paparazzi combined with the speed of the Internet has created an insatiable appetite for gossip fed by a fast lane to stardom for anyone who wanted to jump on and drive.'

In the same year, *Newsweek* magazine carried in a story subtitled 'In defense of our tabloid culture.' It fashioned a persuasive attempt to explicate what was then a new type of figure that was not too close, not too far away, but at the exact distance from audiences from where they could feel a sense of intimacy. 'We have invented celebrity and latched onto it because celebrity does a better job of giving us what traditional art and entertainments once gave us,' went the argument. Celebrities didn't so much tell stories; they *were* stories. We're not talking Dickens or Hemingway here; just stories about recovering from addictions, or broken marriages and so on. Celebrities presented a 'narrative in the medium of life,' as *Newsweek* put it. Between them, the two publications provided a neat summary of culture in the 2000s: gossipy, meritocratic with a population keen to be entertained. The media had reacted to changes in taste and sensibility and harvested intel for public consumption. That was 2009, remember.

In December 2016, the *Guardian* writer Peter Robinson distinguished between the old-fashioned fame, epitomized by Taylor Swift, whose rise was assisted by concerts, records, press and broadcast media and what he called the 'modern type of fame,' originating in and sustained by the digital world. Robinson pondered how Instagram, Twitter and Snapchat had opened up direct lines of communication with audiences, often bypassing traditional channels. The distance between artists and audiences didn't so much close up as disappear. 'Fans can be complicit,' wrote Robinson. Actually, they always *are*; they're involved in the activity of producing and maintaining fame.

Celebrities didn't have to have relatability (that quality again) in the 2000s; today, it's a *sine qua non*: it doesn't matter if audiences are pleased or pissed by a celebrity, just as long as they experience a connection, preferably one that stirs strong emotions. That much is essential. It's as if there's a calculus based on infinitesimal differences between properties that audiences use to determine who's invited to stay and who gets ignored. Social media may not offer wormholes to the soul of celebrities, but it makes some appear imperfectly, fallibly, authentically human and it has, as Robehmed puts it, 'weaponized fame.' It gives them the ammunition to use renown for more utilitarian purposes, the main one being to make money. Robehmed may underestimate the smartness, imagination and all-round savvy of consumers; they know the likes of Kylie Jenner are making millions out of them; they also know that she does so with their approval. Remove that approval and Kylie et al. are consigned to oblivion.

I'm not attempting a circle-squaring feat with this book: I know its arguments will survive only until the next sideswipe takes us all by surprise. Nobody could have seen celebrity culture coming. It was greeted by many as sense-dulling alternative to religion, a capitalist connivance to relieve us of our money, a disempowering symptom of the global corporatization of everything and everyone, and other things beside. We're now accustomed, and almost anaesthetized, to images of people we know, but don't know what for. And being hastened to eBay or some other place where we can shop for the products they recommend.

In a way, the cultural landscape has never been so unsparing: everywhere, it seems, someone is making a grab for our money. Commerce has corrupted culture and used celebrities to do the dirty work. That would be one perspective. When I hear it, I'm reminded of the Ghost Dance, a ritual practiced by an American Indian cult in the late nineteenth century, the followers of which believed that the dance would drive away white people and restore traditional ways of life. The believers wore shirts they thought would make them invulnerable to whites' bullets. Like the ill-fated Ghost Dancers, critics of celebrity culture have discovered that, much as they warn against the baleful consequences of our current fixation on people who make little or no material impact on our well-being, their caveats are useless. Actually, all statements, good or bad, about cultural change are ineffectual: rock 'n' roll, television, smartphones, gambling, gangsta rap, drugs – the list goes on. They've all had their Ghost Dancers.

By now, readers will have realized that the *Kardashian Kulture* of the title is a product of our own making; we experience everything with other people – practically from the moment we're born, actually. What we call culture serves as the context for everything we experience, including our knowledge of the natural world and even ourselves. These experiences are mediated and modified for us by other people; mothers first. As adults a prodigious proportion of our thoughts, hopes, anxieties and projects revolve around other people. Nowadays, those people are often never seen or spoken to directly. And yet their influence is overwhelming.

'How celebrities changed life in the 21st century' is probably the most misleading subtitle I could have dreamt up because celebrities didn't and can't change life. People do. Celebrities are creations rather than people; they're products of imaginations; audiences think they know them but they exist outside time and space and reside only in the imagination. Audiences engage with ideas rather than events; if they discern qualities in someone or something and take an interest in them to the point where they involve themselves in their imagined lives, they make celebrities.

So even celebrities as humongous as the Kardashians can't exist without public recognition. All the same, even imagined celebrities thrill and entrance. What distinguishes today's – and I mean, post-2007 – celebrity culture is the replacement of traditional dichotomies (stars/fans on one side; leaders/

followers on the other) by fluidity. Consumers don't occupy space on one side of a divide because there is no divide.

That butterfly I wrote about in Chapter 1; let's imagine that, at the moment it started to flap its wings, a fascinated child caught it, stopping the flutter that led to the sequence of far-reaching effects. How might this book's timeline be different? Let's imagine, in 1989, Madonna's video for *Like a Prayer* is critically received as an interesting, exotic exercise that addresses several important themes, including religion, race and sexuality, fearlessly and with an intellectual flourish worthy of French art cinema. Pepsi continues to use it in its advertising and Madonna is hailed as a legitimate artist. In three years' time, her book *Sex* draws rapturous reviews and her video for *Justify My Love* is acknowledged as a brave if rarefied essay on passion. By 1996, when Madonna gives birth to her daughter Lourdes Leon, she is 38 and a respectable and often challenging entertainer on the cusp of middle age.

Madonna doesn't crave the kind of attention given to Anna Nicole Smith, whose reality TV show has, for some unaccountable reason, gripped audiences and becomes, in two years, one of the most spectacularly successful TV shows ever. Smith's global fame, one could say notoriety, brings her contracts from everywhere. She signs for Donald Trump's model agency at the same time as Paris Hilton in 2000. Plans for a reality show featuring Hilton intended to rival Smith's are dropped after audience research suggests she'll be annihilated in the viewer ratings. In 2003, the Barbra Streisand case alerts everyone to the power of the consumer when armed to the teeth by the internet. But the appetite to investigate others' private lives isn't that great and, with so much reality television available, audiences can inspect their favored celebrities closely without even touching a QWERTY keyboard.

In 2007, when Anna Nicole Smith dies, all manner of TV projects are abandoned for fear that broadcasters will be seen to be opportunistically trying to fill a void. Among the canceled projects is E!'s proposed reality show focusing on the family descended from Robert Kardashian, the LA lawyer who came to prominence when he helped defend OJ Simpson in 1994. He died in 2003. That's presumably the last we'll hear about the Kardashians.

Perhaps a world in which Madonna's feral instincts — what Camille Paglia called her animalism, as I noted in Chapter 2 — and subversive forays into taboo areas were appreciated politely, things wouldn't have changed as much. A Kardashian-free environment would have materialized, but there would have been other real, self-admiring people, some loveable, others detestable, on our screens to engage us in a way that kept us overextended. I mean overextended in the financial sense, but readers can probably add more ways.

In the event, the real world responded in a way that changed practically everything we take for granted. Today sexagenarian Madonna is often depicted as the great survivor; her spirit and individuality survived and thrived in a culture designed, in the 1980s, to repress. You could see her as Pandora, the girl with all the gifts, who released profound immorality and wickedness or, according to other versions of the myth, blessings. Confessional TV, reality shows, public figures with private lives laid out for public inspection and lines of communication that made voyeurism innocent became defining features of culture. The *dramatis personae* of entertainment expanded as ordinary people came into view, their lives no less interesting than the characters who appeared on stage, or screen.

The Kardashian-free world never materialized. If it hadn't been the Kardashians who opted to live out their lives in full view of the public and, in exchange, asked for only a few hundred million (or a billion in Kylie's case), it would be other 'ordinary' celebs. The relatable ones. Cynics are going to insist that celebrities are part of a delivery mechanism to keep audiences stimulated, craving for new consumer goods and acting impulsively to buy them. I don't dismiss this argument, though, if it hadn't been celebrities, corporations would have found other ways and means of maintaining the rhythm of consumerism that started up in the twentieth century.

"Consumption is a primary means of sanctification, and consumables ranging from perfume, cigarettes, and champagne to film, photography, and celebrity all proffer modern contexts for spiritual and physical rebirth." Shannon McRae, a professor of English, and Colbey Emmerson Reid, the director of a market research consortium, were writing in 2015 about what they called "Cocktail Culture" (which connects tenuously with our front cover design). Commodities are "treated as tangible extensions of our most intimate and transcendent selves."

It's a heady argument and one that's interesting enough to deserve more attention than I'm going to give it here. I just want to emphasize how all of us, readers, reviewers, entertainers, people who love celebrities and those who can't stand them, are all consumers. McRae and Reid are, in my view, right about how we treat products – not so much as things but as extensions, though I'm not sure about sanctification (or spiritual rebirth, for that matter).

Kim Kardashian and her relatives will be remembered; they accompany us as impassive spectators, even though they're hardly impassive. We sense their pain and pleasure as they navigate their ways through divorces, surgery, and legal actions. We can always see them, even if we're invisible to them. We sometimes want to reach out in empathy or fury.

Our eyes roll back at the mention of the name. There's no escaping the Kardashians. Whether you regard the family as a witless bunch of overpaid show-offs or conveyors of the zeitgeist is a matter of judgment and taste. But the impact of the Kardashians is undeniable. It won't please many people. In fact, it probably won't please any at all outside the Kardashian family. But practically everything in popular culture today bears an impression of the Kardashians. This probably means we are already looking at late-phase Kardashians. Considering they came to public notice in 2007, they have enjoyed a barely believable tenure. Celebrity culture is a hazardous place and its attrition rate means celebs are always at the whim of the public's sudden arbitrariness; no one's power to fascinate is inexhaustible. The public tires of everyone eventually.

BIBLIOGRAPHY

BOOKS AND ARTICLES

Allen, T. W. (2012). *The Invention of the White Race, Volume 1: Racial Oppression and Social Control.* London: Verso.

Anderson, D. (1976). Bruce Jenner didn't fail himself. *New York Times.* Retrieved from https://nyti.ms/2mNrTx8. Accessed in July 31, 2018.

Azevedo, A., Drost Ellen, A., & Mullen, M. R. (2002). Individualism and collectivism: Toward a strategy for testing measurement equivalence across culturally diverse groups. *Cross Cultural Management: An International Journal, 9*(1), 19–29.

Bachrach, J. (2013). Zoë Saldana: Her *Allure* photo shoot. *Allure,* May 13. Retrieved from http://bit.ly/2qRMov6. Accessed in April 2018.

Balakrishnan, J., & Griffiths, M. J. (2018). An exploratory study of 'Selfitis' and the development of the Selfitis Behavior Scale. *International Journal of Mental Health Addiction, 16*(3), 722–736.

Baldwin, J. (1984). *Notes of a Native Son*. New York, NY: Beacon Press.

Bauman, Z. (2005). *Liquid Life*. Cambridge: Polity Press.

Bellezza, A., Paharia, N., & Keinan, A. (2016). Conspicuous consumption of time: When busyness and lack of leisure time become a status symbol. *Journal of Consumer Research*, *44*, 119–138.

Bennett, E. (2016). Kim Kardashian pens essay explaining why she isn't a feminist. *Grazia*, August 17. Retrieved from http://bit.ly/2mFPi3r. Accessed in July 2018.

Bennett, L. (1993). *The Shaping of Black America: The Struggles and Triumphs of African-Americans, 1619 to the 1990s*. London: Penguin.

Bissinger, B. (2015). Caitlyn Jenner: The full story. *Vanity Fair*, November 25. Retrieved from http://bit.ly/2qc4B6b. Accessed in April 2018.

Bourdieu, P. (2010). *Distinction*. London: Routledge.

Broughton, P. D. (2016). The sensational reality of life as a Kardashian. *Financial Times*, October 8, p. 11.

Brown, S. (2015). Brands on a wet, black bough: Marketing the masterworks of modernism. *Arts Marketing*, *5*(1), 5–24.

Bruce, L. (2011). The business behind TV's Kardashian wedding: A likely ratings bonanza for *E!*, the Aug. 20 nuptials of Kim Kardashian are a perfect storm of $100,000 ad spots, a $1.5 million photo sale and lots … and lots … of freebies. *Hollywood Reporter*, 26 August. Retrived from http://bit.ly/2DnW8Ao. Accessed in March 2018.

Bruce, T. (2004). Making the boundaries of the 'normal' in televised sports: The play-by-play of race. *Media, Culture, Society*, 26(6), 861–879.

Butcher, L., Phau, I., & Shimul, A. S. (2017). Uniqueness and status consumption in generation Y consumers: Does moderation exist? *Marketing Intelligence & Planning*, 35(5), 673–687. Retrieved from https://doi.org/10.1108/MIP-12-2016-0216. Accessed in February 2018.

Butler, J. (1990). *Gender Trouble*. London: Routledge.

Cal, A. M., & Mallette, L. A. (2015). Celebrity and the United Nations: Leadership and referent power of global film ambassadors. *International Journal of Arts & Sciences*, 8(5), 415–428.

Callahan, E. (2016). Symposium review: Kimposium! A symposium about all things Kardashian, Brunel University London, 26 November 2015. *International Journal of Fashion Studies*, 3(1), 153–155.

Cashmore, E. (2010). *Making Sense of Sports*. Abingdon: Routledge.

Cashmore, E. (2016). *Elizabeth Taylor: A Private Life for Public Consumption*. London/New York, NY: Bloomsbury Publishing.

Cashmore, E., Cleland, J., & Dixon, K. (2018). *Screen Society*. Basingstoke: Palgrave Macmillan.

Caudill, S. B., & Mixon, F. G. Jr. (2012). Celebrity wardrobe malfunctions: Economic efficiency, property rights assignment, and liability in popular culture. *Journal of Economics and Economic Education Research*, 14(2), 37–48.

Cohen, D. (2016). Selfies, narcissism and social media (infographic). *AdWeek*, January 6. Retrieved from http://bit.ly/2I3LCAU. Accessed in June 2018.

Cristini, H., Kauppinen-Räisänen, H., Barthod-Prothade, M., & Woodside, A. (2016). Toward a general theory of luxury: Advancing from workbench definitions and theoretical transformations. *Journal of Business Research*, 70, 101–107.

Cross, S., & Littler, J. (2010). Celebrity and *schadenfreude*: The cultural economy of fame in freefall. *Cultural Studies*, 24(3), 395–417.

Davis, V. (2002). The father of scandal. *British Journalism Review*, 13(4), 74–80.

Deflem, M. (2013). Professor goes Gaga: Teaching Lady Gaga and the sociology of fame. *The American Sociologist*, 44(2), 117–131.

Dosekun, S. (2015). For Western girls only: Post-feminism as transnational culture. *Feminist Media Studies*, 15(6), 960–975.

Driessens, O. (2012). The celebritization of society and culture: Understanding the structural dynamics of celebrity culture. *International Journal of Cultural Studies*, 16(6), 641–657.

Driessens, O. (2013). Celebrity capital: Redefining celebrity using field theory. *Theory and Society*, 42(5), 543–560.

Duffett, M. (2015). Elvis' gospel music: Between the secular and the spiritual? *Religions*, 6(1), 182–203.

Elliott, A. (2010). 'I want to look like that!': Cosmetic surgery and celebrity culture. *Cultural Sociology*, 5(4), 463–477.

Evans, A., & Riley, S. (2013). Immaculate consumption: Negotiating the sex symbol in postfeminist culture. *Journal of Gender Studies, 22*(3), 268–281.

Everett, L. (2016). Why is *Frozen* so popular? You asked Google – Here's the answer. *Guardian*, December 20. Retrieved from http://bit.ly/2EHFhLj. Accessed in February 2018.

Farrow, R. (2017). From aggressive overtures to sexual assault: Harvey Weinstein's accusers tell their stories. *The New Yorker*, October 23, pp. 1–26.

Feldblum, C. R., & Lipnic, V. A. (2016). *Select task force on the study of harassment in the workplace.* Washington, DC: US Equal Opportunities Commission.

Felt, H. (2015). Caitlyn Jenner showed true courage. She fully deserves the world's praise. *Guardian*, July 16. Retrieved from http://bit.ly/2uNh2HZ. Accessed in July 2018.

Fischer, M. (2016). Think gender is performance? You have Judith Butler to thank for that. *New York*, June 13. Retrieved from https://www.sbs.com.au/news/the-feed/you-think-gender-is-performance-you-have-judith-butler-to-thank-for-that. Accessed in April 2018.

Flanagan, C. (2015). 'Selfish', by Kim Kardashian West, and more. *New York Times*, September 22. Retrieved from https://nyti.ms/2JVc0CH. Accessed in June 2018.

Friedman, V. (2017). Pinups in the post-Weinstein world. *New York Times*, November 27. Retrieved from https://nyti.ms/2JSBk8E. Accessed in April 2018.

Funk, S., & Funk, J. (2016). Transgender dispossession in *Transparent*: Coming out as a euphemism for honesty. *Sexuality & Culture*, *20*(4), 879–905.

Furedi, F. (2003). Get off that couch. *Guardian*, October 9. Retrieved from http://bit.ly/VrYo3r. Accessed in June 2018.

Gabler, N. (2001). Toward a new definition of celebrity. Norman Lear Center: University of Southern California, Annenberg. Retrieved from http://bit.ly/-GablerToward NewDef.

Gallagher, C., & Laqueur, T. (Eds.). (1987). *The Making of the Modern Body: Sexuality and Society in the Nineteenth Century*. Berkeley, CA: University of California Press.

Gamson, J. (2011). The unwatched life is not worth living: The elevation of the ordinary in celebrity culture. *Publications of the Modern Language Association of America*, *126*(4), 1061–1069.

Goffman, E. (1990, orig. 1956). *The Presentation of Self in Everyday Life*. London: Penguin.

Goldberg, M. (2014). What is a woman? *The New Yorker*, August 4. Retrieved from http://bit.ly/2qFLJfZ. Accessed in April 2018.

Goldsmith, R. E., Flynn, L. R., & Clark, R. A. (2012). Materialistic, brand engaged and status consuming consumers and clothing behaviors. *Journal of Fashion Marketing and Management: An International Journal*, *16*(1), 102–119. Retrived from http://bit.ly/2EVi1ME. Accessed in February 2017.

Goude, J.-P. (1982). *Jungle Fever*. New York, NY: Farrar Straus & Giroux.

Gurstein, R. (2006). The culture of narcissism revisited. *Salmagundi*, (150/151), 13–24.

Harris, D. (2016a). The Kardashians. *Southwest Review*, *101*(4), 601–613.

Harris, D. (2016b). The sacred androgen: The transgender debate. *Antioch Review*, *Winter*, 64–76.

Hauhart, R. C. (2015). American sociology's investigations of the American dream: Retrospect and prospect. *The American Sociologist*, *46*(1), 65–98.

Hellmueller, L. C., & Aeschbacher, N. (2010). Media and celebrity: Production and consumption of "Well-Knownness". *Communication Research Trends*, *29*(4), 1–35.

Hughes, S. (2015). Kardashians blaze a trail as celebrities seize control of their digital brands. *Guardian*, September 26, p. 33. Retrieved from http://bit.ly/2HsXbBL. Accessed in March 2018.

Hughey, M. W. (2011). The (dis)similarities of white racial identities: The conceptual framework of 'hegemonic whiteness'. *Ethnic and Racial Studies*, *33*(8), 1289–1309.

Ismail, N. (2017). If Rachel Dolezal can be Nkechi Diallo, can I identify as a white girl called Elizabeth at airport security? *Independent*, March 5. Retrieved from https://ind.pn/2JYPTXl. Accessed in July 2018.

Jahr, C. (1976). Elton's frank talk: The lonely love life of a superstar. *Rolling Stone*. Retrieved from https://rol.st/2AdRau0. Accessed in July 2018.

Kapoor, I. (2013). *Celebrity Humanitarianism: The Ideology of Global Charity*. London: Routledge.

Karmali, S. (2017). This is how much the Kardashians get paid for one Instagram post. *Harper's Bazaar*, March 17. Retrived from http://bit.ly/2FLowSz. Accessed in March 2018.

Kedzior, R., & Allen, D. E. (2016). From liberation to control: Understanding the selfie experience. *European Journal of Marketing*, *50*(9–10), 1893–1902.

Kelly, C. (2014). Why we are (still) talking about Kanye West and Kim Kardashian's *Vogue* cover. *Washington Post – Blogs*, March 26.

Klazas, E. B. (2015). Selfhood, citizenship … and all things Kardashian: Neoliberal and postfeminist ideals in reality television. *Media and Communication Studies Summer Fellows*. Paper 2. Retrieved from http://bit.ly/2FVk18R. Accessed in March 2018.

Kniazeva, M., & Babicheva, E. (2017). (Un)saving face, or the designer face as a new consumer commodity. *Journal of Business Research*, *7*(C), 143–148.

Kolbert, E. (2018). There's no scientific basis for race – It's a made-up label. *National Geographic*, April. Retrieved from https://on.natgeo.com/2qH5ROg. Accessed in April 2018.

Kowalczyk, C. M., & Royne, M. B. (2013). The moderating role of celebrity worship on attitudes toward celebrity brand extensions. *Journal of Marketing Theory and Practice*, *21*(2), 211–220.

Lasch, C. (1976). The Narcissist Society. *The New York Review of Books*, September 30. Retrieved from http://bit.ly/2skD5Ex. Accessed in May 2018.

Lasch, C. (1980). *The Culture of Narcissism: American Life in an Age of Diminishing Expectations*. London: Abacus.

Lasch, C. (1991). *The True and Only Heaven: Progress and Its Critics*. New York, NY: W. W. Norton.

Le Vine, L. (2017). Kylie Jenner and the Kardashian sisters caught in cosmetics legal woes. *Vanity Fair*, January 25. Retrieved from http://bit.ly/2ufOrrI. Accessed in August 2017.

Llamas, R., & Thomsen, T. U. (2015). The luxury of igniting change by giving: Transforming yourself while transforming others' lives. *Journal of Business Research*, *69*(1), 166–176.

Llewellyn Smith, J. (2017). When Harry Styles shared a shirt with Tess Ward. *The Australian*, May 17. Retrieved from http://bit.ly/2qvptG1. Accessed in May 2017.

Lueck, J. A. (2015). Friend-zone with benefits: The parasocial advertising of Kim Kardashian. *Journal of Marketing Communications*, *21*(2), 91–109.

Luo, W. (2013). Aching for the altered body: Beauty economy and Chinese consumption of cosmetic surgery. *Women's Studies International Forum*, *38*, 1–10.

MacDonald, P. (2014). Narcissism in the modern world. *Psychodynamic Practice*, *20*(2), 144–153.

Manby, C. (2018). Let's not start a pity party for Jennifer Aniston – She is an icon and deserves to live her best life. *Independent*, February 18. Retrieved from https://ind.pn/2ohPKoU. Accessed in February 2018.

Mansvelt, J. (2010). *Geographies of Consumption*. London: Sage.

Marriott, H. (2014). Why Kim Kardashian deserves to be on the cover of *Vogue*. *Guardian*, March 24. Retrieved from http://bit.ly/2HqOO9M. Accessed in March 2018.

Martens, T. (2014). Name of the game is fame: 'Kim Kardashian: Hollywood' lifts curtain on celebrity lifestyle. *Los Angeles Times/Hero Complex: Pop culture unmasked*, August 2. Retrieved from http://lat.ms/2E8VGIp. Accessed in January 2018.

McDonnell, A. (2012). *Just like us: Celebrity gossip magazines in American popular culture.* PhD Dissertation, Ann Arbor, MI: University of Michigan.

McDonnell, A. (2014). *Reading Celebrity Gossip Magazines.* Cambridge: Polity Press.

McGuigan, L. (2012). Consumers: The commodity product of interactive commercial television, or, is Dallas Smythe's thesis more germane than ever? *Journal of Communication Inquiry*, *36*(4), 288–304.

McRae, S., & Emmerson, C. (2015). Fallen angel: The consumption of religion through American cocktail culture. *Material Religion*, *11*(2), 224–249.

McRobbie, A. (2008). Young women and consumer culture: An intervention. *Cultural Studies*, *22*(5), 531–550.

Merton, R. K. (1938). Social structure and anomie. *American Sociological Review*, *3*(5), 672–682.

Miller, J. (2015). Rihanna praises Rachel Dolezal: 'I think she was a bit of a hero'. *Vanity Fair*, October 6. Retrieved from http://bit.ly/2LFHZai. Accessed in July 2018.

Morrison, P. (2017). Patt Morrison asks: Rachel Dolezal on racial fluidity and her changing identity. *Los Angeles Times*, March 8. Retrived from https://lat.ms/2vNdYOM. Accessed in April 2018.

Nelson Blake, C. (2010). Historian, critic, prophet: Christopher Lasch & the American predicament. *Commonweal*, October 18, pp. 21–28.

Neville, R. D., Gorman, C., Flanagan, S., & Dimanche, F. (2015). Negotiating fitness, from consumption to virtuous production. *Sociology of Sport Journal*, *32*(3), 284–311.

Newsweek Staff. (2018). "Tiger-Stalking" In defense of our tabloid culture. *Newsweek*, December 11. Retrieved from http://bit.ly/Newsceleb. Accessed in July 2018.

Nisbett, G. S., & Childs DeWalt, C. (2016). Exploring the influence of celebrities in politics: A focus group study of young voters. *Atlantic Journal of Communication*, *24*(3), 144–156.

Ofari Hutchinson, E. (2011). Halle Berry custody battle re-opens 'one drop rule' debate. *The Grio*, February 8. Retrieved from https://on.thegrio.com/2qKjGMy. Accessed in April 2018.

Ogunnaike, L. (2005). Paris Inc. *New York Times*, May 2. Retrieved from https://nyti.ms/2KpPXAG. Accessed in May 2018.

Oldenburg, A. (2009). Decade in celebrities: Nobodies walk the path to stardom. *USA Today*, December 31. Retrieved from https://usat.ly/2LiqvR2. Accessed in July 2018.

Opree, S. J., & Kühne, R. (2016). Generation Me in the spotlight: Linking reality TV to materialism, entitlement, and narcissism. *Mass Communication and Society*, *19*(6), 800–819.

Orth, M. (2000). *Vulgar favors: Andrew Cunanan, Gianni Versace and the largest failed manhunt in the US history*. New York, NY: Bantam Doubleday.

Oudshoorn, N. (1994). *Beyond the Natural Body: An Archeology of Sex Hormones.* London: Routledge.

Paglia, C. (1990). Madonna – Finally, a real feminist. *New York Times*, December 14. Retrieved from https://nyti. ms/2JMYPjy. Accessed in April 2018.

Paper [sic]. (2014). Break the Internet Kim Kardashian. *PAPER*, November 11 (Winter). Retrieved from http://bit.ly/ 2NRi5Of. Accessed in July 2018.

Paton, E. (2016). Kylie Jenner and the year of the drop. *New York Times*, December 14. Retrieved from http://nyti. ms/2pnKQY4. Accessed in March 2018.

Patsiaouras, G. (2017). The history of conspicuous consumption in the United Kingdom: 1945–2000. *Journal of Historical Research in Marketing*, 9(4), 488–510.

People Team. (2012). Kanye and Kim: Personal or business? *USA Today*, International edition, April 17. Retrieved from http://bit.ly/2K573T7. Accessed in July 2018.

Petrarca, E. (2017). Paris Hilton invented everything you're doing in 2017, and she knows it. *W*, May 10. Retrieved from http://bit.ly/2Ietc5w. Accessed in May 2018.

Philipsen, D. (2003). '… One of those evils that will be very difficult to correct': The permanence of race in North America. *Journal of Negro Education*, 72(2), 190–207.

Pinksy, D., & Young, S. M. (2009). *The Mirror Effect: How Celebrity Narcissism is Seducing America.* New York, NY: Harper.

Pisani, L. (2015). Women and selfie culture: The selfie as a feminist communication tool. *Journalism Interest Group, CCA/Groupe d'intérêt en journalisme, ACC*, Retrieved from http://cca.kingsjournalism.com/?cat=7. Accessed in March 2018.

Proulx, M. (2015). There is no more social media — Just advertising. *AdAge*, April 2. Retrieved from http://bit.ly/2rB1aqq. Accessed in Many 2018.

Pullman, L. (2018). Sleaze in the city: And now it's our turn, boys. *Sunday Times*, January 28, p. 24.

Reich, W. (1979, orig. 1927). *The Function of the Orgasm*. New York, NY: Farrar, Straus and Giroux.

Riddle, K., & De Simone, J. J. (2013). A snooki effect? An exploration of the surveillance subgenre of reality TV and viewers' beliefs about the 'real' real world. *Psychology of Popular Media Culture*, 2(4), 237–250.

Riviere, S. (2015). The Kardashian sisters are the true heirs to The Brontës. *Telegraph*, May 5. Retrieved from http://bit.ly/2DMgNyr. Accessed in April 2018.

Robehmed, N. (2018). How 20-year-old Kylie Jenner built a $900 million fortune in less than 3 years. *Forbes*, July 11. Retrieved from http://bit.ly/2uDWv7W. Accessed in July 2018.

Robinson, P. (2016). How the fame game changed in 2016. *Guardian*, December 21. Retrieved from http://bit.ly/2BssngQ. Accessed in January 2018.

Rosenberg, A. (2014). Kim Kardashian is the perfect celebrity for the outrage age. *Washington Post — Blogs*, November 18. Retrieved from http://wapo.st/2FfsaQF. Accessed in January 2018.

Rubinoff, J. (2011). In defence of Kim Kardashian: We have seen the celebrity enabler and the enabler is us. *Toronto Star*, November 26, section E12.

Ryan, H., & Tschorn, A. (2010). The Kardashian spell: Defying odds, their pop empire keeps growing. *Los Angeles Times*, February 19, section A1. Retrieved from https://lat.ms/2Ool4ic. Accessed in July 2018.

Ryan, M. (2015). Entertaining fantasies: Lifestyle and social life in 1980s America. *Journal of Communication Inquiry*, *39*(1), 82–101.

Sanders, M., & Tamma, F. (2015). The science behind why people give money to charity. *Guardian*, March 23. Retrieved from http://bit.ly/2Mzfmco. Accessed in June 2018.

Schiebinger, L. (1987). Skeletons in the closet: The first illustrations of the female skeleton in eighteenth-century anatomy. In C. Gallagher & T. Laqueur (Eds.), *The Making of the Modern Body: Sexuality and Society in the Nineteenth Century*. Berkeley, CA: University of California Press.

Schiebinger, L. (1989). *The Mind Has No Sex: Women in the Origins of Modern Science*. Cambridge, MA: Harvard University Press.

Schuessler, J. (2015). The term 'African-American' appears earlier than thought: Reporter's notebook. *New York Times*, April 21. Retrieved from https://nyti.ms/2JYhauf. Accessed in April 2018.

Scott, W. D. (2012; orig. 1913). *The Psychology of Advertising: A Simple Exposition of the Principles of Psychology in Their Relation to Successful Advertising*. London: Forgotten Books.

Shelley, S. (2017). Out-of-control panhandling needs a national solution. *Los Angeles Daily News*, July 18. Retrieved from http://bit.ly/2tcenqw. Accessed in June 2017.

Shinn, P. (2015). How Bruce Jenner became the 'World's Greatest Athlete'. *TeamUSA.org*, April 30. Retrieved from https://go.teamusa.org/2GA6Yd4. Accessed in April 2017.

Siegel, L. (2010). The book of self-love: Narcissism. *New York Times*, February 5. Retrieved from http://nyti.ms/2poygrG. Accessed in March 2018.

Simon, R. L. (2016). Moral narcissism and the least-great generation. *Commentary*, May 19, pp. 18–21.

Slide, A. (2010). *Inside the Hollywood Fan Magazine: A History of Star Makers, Fabricators, and Gossip Mongers*. Jackson, MS: University Press of Mississippi.

Snell Herzog, P., & Price, H. E. (2016). *American Generosity: Who Gives and Why*. Oxford: Oxford University Press.

Spickard, P. (1997). Review of *Neither Black Nor White Yet Both: Thematic Explorations of Interracial Literature* by Werner Sollors and *The New Colored People: The Mixed Race Movement in America* by Jon Michael Spencer. *Journal of American Ethnic History*, *18*(2), 153–156.

Sporn, N. (2018). Sir Elton John isn't a fan of *Love Island* celebrities who don't 'work for their stardom'. *Evening Standard*, May 9. Retrieved from http://bit.ly/2jKVqGd. Accessed in May 2018.

St John Kelly, E. (1998). Springer's harvest. *New York Times*, April 27. Retrieved from https://nyti.ms/2Kpsoec. Accessed in June 2018.

Stearns, P. N. (2014). Review of *The Americanization of Narcissism* by Elizabeth Lunbeck. *Journal of Interdisciplinary History*, *45*(2), 252–253.

Stinson, F. S., Dawson, D. A., Goldstein, R. B., Chou, S. P., Huang, B., Smith, S., … Grant, B. F. (2008). Prevalence, correlates, disability, and comorbidity of DSM-IV narcissistic personality disorder: Results from the wave 2 national epidemiological survey on alcohol and related conditions. *Journal of Clinical Psychiatry*, 69(7), 1033–1045.

Streiff, M., & Dundes, L. (2017). Frozen in time: How Disney gender-stereotypes its most powerful princess. *Social Sciences*, 6(38), Retrieved from http://bit.ly/2OyS6vY. Accessed in August 2018.

Stuart Parramore, L. (2016). How America became the love child of Kim Kardashian and Donald Trump. *Reuters*, February 24. Retrived from http://reut.rs/2tvdxHY Accessed in March 2018.

Telegraph Reporters. (2016). Women are changing how they speak 'to sound like Kim Kardashian'. *Telegraph*, April 27. Retrieved from http://bit.ly/2vCp7x0. Accessed in July 2017.

Tiidenberg, K. (2018). *Selfies: Why We Love (and Hate) Them*. Bingley: Emerald.

Tilley, C. (2011). Halle Berry: 'My daughter is black'. *BBC World Service*. Retrieved from https://bbc.in/2LtzlfF. Accessed in July 2018.

Tolentino, J. (2016). How 'empowerment' became something for women to buy. New York Times Magazine, April 12, p. MM23.

van de Rijt, A., Shor, E., Ward, C., & Skiena, S. (2013). Only 15 minutes? The social stratification of fame in the printed media. *American Sociological Review*, 78(2), 266–289.

Vargas-Cooper, N. (2017). Womanhood redefined: A feminist's take on the transgender controversy. *The American Conservative*, January/February, 27–32.

Vider, S. (2012). *Hollywood Bohemians: Transgressive Sexuality and the Selling of the Movieland Dream. Journal of the History of Sexuality*, 21(3), 548–550.

Ward, T. (2015). *The Naked Diet*. London: Quadrille Publishing.

Warde, A. (2015). The sociology of consumption: Its recent development. *Annual Review of Sociology*, 41, 117–134. Retrieved from http://bit.ly/2oqGUGo. Accessed in February 2017.

Weeks, J. (2003). *Sexuality*. (2nd ed.). London: Routledge.

White, S. (2016). A short treatise on narcissism: From normal to risk for violence. *Work Trauma Services Newsletter*, Fall.

Williams, J. (2006). Confessional culture. In W. G. Staples (Ed.), *Encyclopedia of Privacy (Vol. 1: A-M*, pp. 116–117). Santa Barbara, CA: Greenwood Publishing.

Winick, C. (1961). Celebrities' errancy as a subject for journalism: A study of *Confidential. International Communication Gazette*, 7(4), 329–334.

Wiseman, E. (2018). They told me I was too fat. *Observer Magazine*, January 28, 12–16.

Wohlfert, L. (1979). When Disco Queen Grace Jones lamented 'I need a man', artist Jean Paul Coude prowled too near her cage. *People*, April 23. Retrived from http://bit.ly/2F7plAI. Accessed in April 2018.

Wolf, N. (2002, orig. 1990). *The Beauty Myth: How Images of Beauty Are Used Against Women*. New York, NY: HarperCollins.

Wolf, N. (2016). Emily Ratajkowski's naked ambition. *Harper's Bazaar*, August. Retrieved from http://bit.ly/2ucx0NS. Accessed in December 2017.

Wycislo, W. E. (2000). Narcissism and Tyranny. *The Classical Bulletin*, 76(1), 71–80.

Yahr, E. (2015). The forgotten history of Bruce Jenner: How the 1970s all-American hero ended up here. *Washington Post*, February 4. Retrieved from https://wapo.st/2AjKhrc. Accessed in July 2018.

Zaharie, M. M., & Maniu, A. I. (2012). How could children become bad consumers – Materialistic values and ethics. *The Proceedings of the International Conference, Marketing – From Information to Decision*. Retrieved from http://bit.ly/2EQzIg9. Accessed in February 2018.

FILMS

9–5 (USA, 1980) directed by Colin Higgins.

10 (USA, 1979) directed by Blake Edwards.

All About Eve (USA, 1950) directed by Joseph L. Mankiewicz.

American Gigolo (USA, 1980) directed by Paul Schrader.

Back to the Future (USA, 1985) directed by Robert Zemeckis.

Conan the Barbarian (USA, 1982) directed by John Milius.

Dangerous (USA, 1935) directed by Alfred E. Green.

Frozen (USA, 2013) directed by Chris Buck and Jennifer Lee.

Gaslight (USA, 1944) directed by George Cukor. Based on Patrick Hamilton's 1938 play of the same name. Retrieved from http://bit.ly/-Gaslight Accessed in July 2018.

House of Wax (Australia/USA, 2005) directed by Jaume Collet-Serra.

Klute (USA, 1971) directed by Alan J. Pakula.

Madonna: Truth or Dare (USA, 1991) directed by Alek Keshishian.

Nina (USA, 2016) directed by Cynthia Mort.

Othello (UK, 1965) directed by Stuart Burge. Based on William Shakespeare's 1622 play of the same name.

Pumping Iron (USA, 1977) directed by George Butler and Robert Fiore.

The Bodyguard (USA, 1992) directed by Mick Jackson.

The Curse (USA/Italy, 1987) directed by David Keith.

The Danish Girl (UK/USA/Germany/Denmark/Belgium, 2015) directed by Tom Hooper.

The Evil Dead (USA, 1981) directed by Sam Raimi.

The Man Who Could Work Miracles, (UK, 1936) directed by Lothar Mendes and produced by Alexander Korda. Based on HG Well's 1898 novel of the same name. Retrieved from http://bit.ly/-Miracles Accessed in July 2018.

The Ring (USA/Japan, 2002) directed by Gore Verblnski.

The Terminator (USA, 1984) directed by James Cameron.

Touch of Evil (USA, 1958) directed by Orson Welles. Based on Whit Masterson's 1956 novel *Badge of Evil*.

Unsane (USA, 2018) directed by Steven Soderbergh.

INDEX